Praise for Unwritten Rules

Lynn Harris has written a lucid, clear-eyed analysis of the barriers facing women's career advancement at the most senior levels and she gives excellent advice on how to navigate around those barriers. This book provides the most astute insights I've yet seen into the elusive but vitally important unwritten rules. Every business school should make this required reading, and it is a must-read for any woman who is serious about her career.

Stephanie MacKendrick
President
Canadian Women In Communications

This impressive book does a phenomenal job at opening one's eyes to the realities of why gender inequality still exists at the highest levels in our organizations and gives highly practical guidance to women who want to succeed in this environment. It is a must read, not only for women seeking management and leadership positions, but also for men who want to make a positive difference in their corporate cultures.

Susan Cordts
President/CEO
Adaptive Technologies, Inc.

Lynn Harris has demystified the challenges facing women who aspire to corner offices in large organizations. Her book is structurally sound, clear, and rational. It's also teeming with examples from people's personal experiences that bring life to the book. This is a roadmap for corporations that wish to mine the wealth of talented women within their organizations and a first-time look at "corporate refugees", women who find success on their own terms. This is an important and valuable resource for the development of women leaders. It is a stellar achievement.

Joan Jenkinson
Executive Producer
S-VOX: VisionTV | One: the Body, Mind & Spirit channel | Joytv 10 & 11

This is a book that every woman who aspires to the C-Suite or boardroom will not be able to put down. It is packed with facts and advice, extremely well researched, written with a good sense of humor and dose of pragmatism. For those women who are considering changing course from the traditional route to the top, there are also some great insights from those who have left that world far behind.

Diane Morris
President
The International Alliance For Women.

Lynn Harris demystifies the structural arches that still support the enduring "glass ceiling" and provides a coherent and functional framework of the thinking and behaviors that foster success for women aspiring to leadership roles in today's organizations. This book provides a core of understanding, in the form of practical contexts and language, that stimulates confidence and managerial courage, regardless of gender. An energizing read and indispensable as a management and leadership reference tool.

May Scally
General Manager
Labplas Inc.

In Unwritten Rules Lynn Harris expresses in clear and understandable terms the issues and their underlying causes that women face everyday in the work place. She gives us invaluable insight into the simple and yet complex and divergent choices that women have to make to succeed.

Mackie I. Vadacchino
CEO- Bioforce Canada Inc.

Unwritten Rules

What Women Need To Know About
Leading In Today's Organizations

LYNN HARRIS

To Paul Arnold
We miss you very much

ACKNOWLEDGEMENTS

Sincere thanks to my gorgeous husband, Jeff Arnold, whose unconditional love and support enrich my life and my work every day. Also, thanks to my friends Tom Costello, whose catalytic intervention helped me overcome my inertia to start writing; Catherine Vaughan, who gave early support and encouragement; and Beth Massiano, whose generous feedback sparked the title for this book. And thanks to all of the women (and my two token men, Gord Cooper and Karim Salabi), who gave their time to be interviewed and who shared their personal stories. And finally, thanks to my wonderful son, Josh Harris, who makes it easy for me to love being a mother (most of the time!).

TABLE OF CONTENTS

INTRODUCTION

Although extensive research has concluded that women have the desire and competence to lead in business, government, education, law, and the social sector, there are still relatively few women at the top of organizations. Theories abound about why this is so. Some think it's because women lack the relevant qualifications and experience to succeed senior male leaders. Others claim that women do not have the inborn psychological traits necessary for good leadership. And more recently, as a few high-profile women have resigned their top jobs, the media questions whether men are more ambitious for power and whether women, despite their claims to the contrary, don't really want it.

There is certainly no shortage of advice, much of it contradictory, for those women who do want to succeed to the top of organizations: women need to be more assertive, but not so assertive that they are disliked; women need to be collaborative, but not so friendly that they lack credibility; women need to be more competent than their male colleagues, but in a way that does not threaten them; and women leaders need to be role models for other women, but need to behave more like men to succeed. Women obviously also need a good sense of humor.

It's hard for women to know how to respond given the advice they are receiving. If they model their behavior on successful male leaders, they are criticized and rejected for being too tough and unfeminine. If they behave authentically as women, they are often considered unsuitable leadership material. Reacting and responding to such well-meaning advice usually has little positive impact and, so far, has not resulted in anything near equal representation in the boardroom or the corner office. If more women are to succeed at the top, we need to understand the *unwritten rules* behind the popular theories that explain the often-inhospitable organizational environment in which women strive to become leaders.

What are the dynamic forces in play that explain why there are so few women leaders at the top of organizations and what, if anything, can women do about them? If you are a woman who aspires to lead, no matter what sector or type of organization, it is essential to know the answer to this question. This is not optional or "nice to have" if you are serious about leading within the current leadership framework. A lack of understanding of the organizational environment and its *unwritten rules* is an ignorance that you simply can't afford. It's like having a snake in the room with the lights turned off—you never know when you might trip over it or get bitten, sometimes fatally. This book turns on the lights, revealing where the organizational snakes are hiding, when and why they are likely to strike, and how to manage or avoid them altogether. Arming yourself with a clearer understanding of the obstacles that female leaders must navigate will position you more strategically in your career and enable you to make better-informed choices about your leadership style and professional development.

This book is in three sections: Section One answers the question of why there are so few women at the top of organizations and reveals the *unwritten rules*—critical information that women need to know about today's organizational environments. Section Two uses this understanding to provide pragmatic solutions about how women need to develop themselves to progress within this context and how to succeed within the *unwritten rules* that show little sign of changing. And for those who question their desire to stay in the world of large organizations, Section Three provides a stimulating exploration into the worlds of women who have become "corporate refugees," leaving their traditional organizational jobs behind to successfully express their leadership capabilities in different arenas.

Section One
Where Are All the Women?

INTRODUCTION

I heard a story about a new CEO of a Fortune 500 company who walked into his initial senior management meeting and his first words were, "Where are all the women?" It's a good question and one that isn't really that difficult to answer.

Section One of this book describes the organizational landscape that women need to navigate if they want to become senior leaders. It confronts and answers the question: Why are there relatively few women at the top of organizations? It then explores what would need to change to enable more women to succeed in this environment. Chapter One provides a big-picture summary of the progress women have made and where they stand now in terms of achieving positions of power at the top of organizations. Chapter Two reveals the *unwritten rules* and explains how they continue to create norms of leadership behavior and a hostile environment for women who want to lead. And Chapter Three looks at the prospects for change that would enable more women to become senior leaders, if that's what they choose.

As a reader of this book, you probably either aspire to be, or already are, a senior leader in an organization, or you are interested in supporting women to lead. You might also be questioning and deciding your future career direction. Given your aspirations and the decisions ahead of you, it is essential to know current reality in relation to the end results that you want to achieve. Without knowing where you are now, it is difficult to make good choices that take you in a direction that is right for you. This understanding of organizational culture and the *unwritten rules* that create the norms of leadership behavior is essential. Without it you are likely to be frequently surprised and frustrated by the obstacles you encounter.

The research data used throughout this book is predominantly from North America and Europe because this is where the interest currently lies for studies of women and leadership.

Chapter One

Demolishing the Concrete Wall and Cracking the Glass Ceiling

Many women today have either forgotten—or have never known—that it wasn't until the beginning of the twentieth century that women were finally allowed to vote. Clearly, we have come a long way in the last hundred years. As recently as the 1970s, there was a metaphorical "concrete wall" that prevented women's access to elite educational institutions, positions in government, the judicial system, and organizational roles other than secretaries and clerks. Women were deemed unsuitable for professional positions in management, academia, accounting, law and other professional fields. President Richard Nixon typified the cultural views of the day when, in 1971, he said, "I don't think a woman should be in any government job whatsoever.... The reason why I do is mainly because they are erratic...and emotional. Men are erratic and emotional, too, but the point is a woman is more likely to be."[1]

The concrete wall metaphor was founded on the widely accepted view that a woman's place was in the home. A survey in a 1965 *Harvard Business Review* quoted one business executive's widely shared opinion that: "The majority of American men and women still believe in home and family, so it is necessary that only one person in the family pursue a career. Because of women's biological role, it is more practical for the man to hold that one position."[2]

Attitudes and practices began to change during the 1970s and, over the next twenty years, the prevailing metaphor evolved from a "concrete wall" to a "glass ceiling." Women achieved access to lower-level positions of authority, but were still excluded from real positions of power at the top of organizations. The glass ceiling metaphor was introduced in a 1986 *Wall Street Journal* article by Carol Hymowitz and Timothy Schellhard, in which they wrote: "Even those women who rose steadily through the ranks eventually crashed into an invisible barrier. The executive suite seemed within their grasp, but they just couldn't break through the glass ceiling."[3]

A 1995 U.S. Congress commission report set up to investigate the so-called glass ceiling phenomenon identified discrimination against higher-level career opportunities for women based predominantly on the belief that women might resign from their jobs to raise a family. This concept continued to penalize women who aspired and were qualified to ascend to positions of authority in all sectors. The glass ceiling was firmly in place and seemed unbreakable.

Then in 2004, Carol Hymowitz reported once again for the *Wall Street Journal* that the glass ceiling had, in effect, been smashed. Her report, *Through the Glass Ceiling*, identified fifty successful executive women "making their mark on the corporate front lines."[4] There was much optimism that significant breakthroughs were being made by some women at the top of organizations that would open a path for others to follow. Given that these women had found a way through to the executive suite, the glass ceiling metaphor no longer seemed to work. But it is hardly the case that the ceiling has been smashed. In 2009, at the time of writing this book, the percentage of women in real positions of power is still very small. Few women are getting jobs where they can influence the policy, strategy, and culture of corporations, government, or academia, even though research continues to support their ability and aspirations to do so.

Today, women continue to be well represented in middle-management positions, both in North America and Europe. According to United Nations data, 42 percent of "legislators, senior officials, and managers" in the United States are women, with a similar picture in Europe with

37 percent in Germany, 33 percent in the United Kingdom, 30 percent in Sweden, and 32 percent in Spain.[5] It's a somewhat different picture, however, when we look at the top jobs where the rate of change continues to be painfully slow and is perhaps even stalling.

In the United States, the percentage of Fortune 500 board seats held by women has increased from 9.6 percent in 1995 to 14.8 percent in 2007.[6] The percentage of Fortune 500 corporate officer positions held by women has followed a similar track from 8.7 percent in 1995 to 15.4 percent in 2007.[7] Canada reports the percentage of Financial Post 500 board seats held by women as 6.2 percent in 1998 rising to 13 percent in 2007. The percentage of Financial Post corporate officer positions held by women in Canada rose from 12 percent in 1999 to 15.1 percent in 2006.[8] However, the most recent Canadian survey of top corporate jobs shows that the number of women in these jobs is actually declining, with a 16 percent decline between 2006 and 2009.[9] The picture in Europe is of even smaller numbers of senior women with the percentage of women on boards in the top three hundred European companies at 8 percent in 2004 rising to 9.7 percent in 2008. Of a total 5,146 board seats in these European countries, women occupied 501.[10]

This picture is little different in government and academia. In the 110th U.S. Congress, women held 16 (16 percent) of the 100 Senate seats and 71 (16.3 percent) of the 435 seats in the House of Representatives.[11] In the thirty-ninth Canadian Parliament, 65 of the 308 seats (21.1 percent) were held by women and, in the 2008 United Kingdom Parliament, women held 126 (19.5 percent) of the 646 seats.[12] In academia, women held only 23 percent of president positions at all United States colleges in 2006.[13]

We could examine more statistics, but they all essentially paint a similar picture. Some women have been skilled and determined enough to find cracks in the glass ceiling and now hold positions at the top of organizations, but they are few and far between. We hear high-profile names, such as Carly Fiorina (former CEO, Hewlett-Packard), Meg Whitman (CEO, eBay), and Anne Mulcahy (former CEO, Xerox), but the fact that we even know their names is an indication of how rare they are. The question of why there are still so few women at the top is exercising the minds of many who are interested in both equal access for women and in the healthy future of organizations.

Prevailing theories

There is no shortage of theories about why there are so few women at the top of organizations. Here are six of the most popular:

1. Lack of women in the executive pipeline

One common explanation, often cited by board members and chief executive officers (CEOs), is that there is a lack of women in the executive pipeline who are qualified to become either C-level directors or board members. It is true that women have lacked experience in line positions, the roles that generate company profits, like sales, manufacturing, and operations, roles that generally lead to promotion to top corporate positions. Women have been, and are still, traditionally concentrated in staff positions, such as human resources, public relations, and accounting. We have to ask ourselves: Why it is that women either choose or are directed into staff rather than line positions? It is particularly puzzling given the fact that, since 1975 in the United States, there has been a dramatic increase in women achieving law degrees and MBAs, qualifications that most commonly provide access to political and organizational leadership. At the last count in 2005 in the United States, women had achieved 49 percent of law degrees and 42 percent of MBAs. They also achieved 57 percent of bachelor's degrees, 59 percent of master's degrees and 48 percent of PhDs.[14] In fact, there is a global trend in the growing educational advantage in women achieving qualifications that should position them well for either line or staff positions.

Although it remains true that woman are concentrated in staff rather than line positions and that women earn fewer degrees than men in many technical and scientific fields, the executive pipeline can no longer be described as devoid of women. There are increasing numbers of women who are experienced and qualified and are still left waiting in the wings and are not getting the top jobs in any significant numbers. It also doesn't explain why, as one woman executive wrote, "Women have been shunted off into support areas for the last thirty years, rather than being in the business of doing business..." [15]

It's not just the C-Suite that lacks significant female representation. Many boards are coming under increasing pressure from stakeholders to increase female membership. The perceived difficulty in finding suitable female candidates for board positions is likely to be at least partly due to the well-entrenched tradition of seeking board directors from the "old boys' network." A July 2009 article in the *Globe and Mail*, Canada's leading newspaper, not only highlights this problem, but suggests two possible solutions:

Dear Susan,

I head the nomination committee for our corporate board of directors. We are seeking candidates to fill two posts that will be vacant later this year. We already have one female director, and are under pressure from stakeholders to increase female representation on the board. But we're having trouble finding qualified candidates with experience in our industry. Advice?

—Name Withheld

Dear Name,

There's no doubt that the current gene pool for corporate directors is too small. Two ideas come to mind.

First, start looking in novel places for new blood instead of always fishing from the same pond. Restricting yourself to the places male board members are usually sought—stretched-thin CEOs and those with prior board experience in your industry—is akin to religious leaders seeking new converts among people who already dress, eat, and think exactly the way they do.

Instead, I suggest looking for female board members where you're most likely to find them—in the public and nonprofit sectors. Twice to three times as many female as male lawyers, for instance, work in government and the not-for-profit sector, according to Ronit Dinovitzer, a sociologist at the University of Toronto, and, while figures were not available, I'd hazard a similar split in other professions too.

If there's a hole in the expertise of your current board, why not look for qualified professional women with transferable skills outside your industry?

Quebec premier Jean Charest used this strategy when he plucked Kathleen Weil, a furloughed lawyer and a rookie MNA, as his justice minister in December. It was her first time in public office, but she had nearly twenty years of experience in the volunteer and nonprofit sectors, directing social and community agencies and sitting on or chairing the boards of huge, fractious health and charitable foundations ... .

This brings me to my second point. You need goodwill, a good strategy and, perhaps most importantly, a good recruiting firm to increase female representation. I learned this from Guylaine Saucier, a chartered accountant who is a corporate director for Petro-Canada, Axa Insurance, Bank of Montreal, Dannon Co., and Areva, and a former chairman of the board of the CBC.

"If you go to a good search firm and tell them this is the kind of expertise we need, you'll find women," she said in a telephone interview from Paris, where she was attending international board meetings for several of these companies."

Still, neither Ms. Saucier nor a new governance group she's advising, The Institute for Governance of Private and Public Organizations, believes in forcing the issue. A recent report by the institute advises ramping up Canadian female board memberships to 40 per cent from 15 percent, but suggests that companies do so at their own pace ... [16]

Rather than there being a lack of women to fill the executive pipeline, there are, in fact, many women who are qualified to succeed to positions at the top of organizations. They might not, however, fit the traditional profile and will certainly not be found within the old boys' network.

2. Women are not genetically programmed to lead

Some believe that the slow rate at which women are ascending to executive positions is because, unlike men, women are not genetically programmed to lead or do not have the inborn psychological traits necessary for good leadership. This theory, put forward by evolutionary psychologists, originates from the claim that male dominance stems from traits that are built into men through adaptation to the primeval environments in which humans evolved. These traits manifest themselves currently, it is claimed, in the aggressive, competitive, controlling, and status-driven behaviors associated with leadership at the top of today's organizations. If these traits were truly inherent in men and not women, it would forever limit women's potential as leaders under this leadership model.

The evolution of stereotypical male and female behavior could, however, equally derive from the types of roles played by women and men within societies. This would mean that the behaviors associated with organizational leadership are not, in fact, inherent but rather learned as part of adaptation to specific roles that men and women fulfill. In contemporary society these roles have changed dramatically: medical advances have given women greater control and choice over reproduction and in their roles as mothers and homemakers; and occupations have undergone a dramatic change with few high-status occupations now favoring men's physical size and power. Biological and social barriers have been reduced, enabling large numbers of women to attain high-status roles in our societies. Role theory, therefore, counters the evolutionary argument that women are not genetically programmed to lead and, in fact, cites research findings that women have been gaining in assertiveness and dominance as their roles have been changing.[17]

If senior leadership positions in today's organizations do require the personality traits of aggression and competitiveness and a desire for control and status, it is likely that women can adapt as required. I have certainly come across female leaders who operate within competitive and aggressive organizational cultures and who demonstrate that they are equally capable of holding their own in such environments. It is questionable, however, if good leadership has anything to do with these traits. Current thinking on effective leadership emphasizes the need for excellent people skills, integrity, authenticity, openness, follow-through, intelligence, and extroversion. Within this context research shows that men and women differ little in the traits and abilities that are most relevant to good leadership, with women generally advantaged on some aspects and men on others.[18]

3. Men are more committed and ambitious for power

Others have agued that men are more committed to their organizations and are more ambitious for power. In 2003, *Fortune Magazine* ran an article questioning whether women really want power: "Many fast-track women are surprisingly ambivalent about what's next. Dozens of powerful women we interviewed tell us that they don't want to be Carly Fiorina ... many don't want to run a huge company." [19] Also in 2003, the *New York Times Magazine* presented a similar article with the provocative headlines: "Q: Why don't more women get to the top? A: They choose not to—Abandoning the climb and heading home." [20] Since then, journalistic debates have continued with a mixture of optimism and pessimism about whether or not women are as dedicated as men to their companies.

Extensive research reveals, however, that there is no difference between men and women in feeling committed to their companies[21] and that the desire for power has proven to be equally strong between the sexes. The only significant difference is that women see power as more interdependent and cooperative, and men construe it as more hierarchical and competitive.[22] And where women have left the career track to senior leadership, they have often made that choice out of frustration with existing opportunities or extended what they intended to be a brief career break only when lacking options to re-enter full-time work.

4. Women leaders are not as effective as male leaders

Could it be that women leaders are simply not as effective as male leaders? This is undoubtedly true in some circumstances, just as it is true that men leaders are not as effective as women leaders in other circumstances. Research shows that leader effectiveness is situational and appears to correlate quite closely with gender stereotypes. In other words, women generally outperform men in leadership positions that are perceived as stereotypically female, and men generally exceed women in stereotypical male roles.[23] Our often unconsciously held stereotypes might have more to do with the perceived effectiveness of men and women leaders, rather than their actual ability to perform a role.

5. Sex-role stereotyping

The underutilization of women's talent in senior leadership roles is often blamed on gender stereotyping. Stereotypes are shortcuts or generalizations that allow us to make sense of our complex world. Gender stereotypes are widely shared views on what is considered appropriate and effective behavior for men and women. There is no doubt that gender stereotyping is alive and well in organizations and throughout societies in general. There is also little question that such stereotyping creates obstacles for women that are difficult to overcome. (In a different way, they also create difficulties for men, but that's a subject for a different book). Catalyst, the North American-based research organization working to advance women in business, produced a report in 2007 examining the impact of gender stereotyping in business.[24] They identified three key predicaments for women:

1) Gender stereotyping leads to extreme perceptions of women in business in that they are either "too soft, too tough and never just right." When women behave in ways that are aligned with female stereotypes, they are judged as less competent leaders (too soft). When women behave in ways that are not aligned with female stereotypes, they are viewed as unfeminine (too tough).

2) Women leaders are held to higher standards and get lower rewards than male leaders. They found that women leaders have to continually prove that they can lead; and at the same time manage stereotypical expectations (too tough or too soft).

3) Women leaders can be competent or likable, but rarely both: "When women behave in ways that are traditionally valued for leaders (e.g., assertively), they tend to be seen as competent, but also not as effective interpersonally as women who adopt a more stereotypically feminine style."[25]

Consequently, gender stereotyping creates a double-bind dilemma for women. If they meet expectations about how they are supposed to behave as women, they are seen as unsuitable leadership material; if they meet expectations about how leaders are supposed to behave, they are viewed as "bully broads," "dragon ladies," or "men in women's clothing" (all descriptions I have personally encountered about women in business). As the Catalyst report concludes, "Women are damned if they do; doomed if they don't."

The real question is not whether gender stereotyping exists, because it clearly does. A more revealing question is whether gender stereotyping is causal to the lack of women at the top of organizations. On its own, I don't think it is. In my view, it is only one of the forces in play in today's organizations that makes it more difficult for women than men, but more of that later.

6. Women don't ask for what they want or promote themselves

It is often said that women don't achieve top jobs or top salaries because they expect to be recognized for their merits without promoting themselves and without being clear with their organizational superiors what it is they want. In my experience of coaching both men and women in organizations, this stereotype is largely true— men are generally much better at asking for what they want and surprise, surprise, then go on to get it more often than women. Linda Babcock and Sara Laschever have explored this behavior in their book *Women Don't Ask. The High Cost of Avoiding Negotiation—and Positive Strategies for Change.*[26] One of their conclusions is that "until society accepts that it is a good thing for women to promote their own interests and negotiate on their own behalf, women will continue to find it difficult to pursue their dreams and ambitions in straightforward and effective ways."

Just like gender stereotyping, avoiding negotiation and self-promotion is a reality for women that certainly hinder their progress to the top jobs, but it is hardly surprising behavior given the gender stereotypes ingrained in our society. If women act on advice to become more assertive and actively promote themselves, they are likely to be judged as too pushy, too tough, or, like Hillary Clinton, who, during her campaign for the Democratic presidential nomination, was accused of trying too hard to be "the smartest girl in the room."[27] It makes sense that women aren't good at self-promotion or stating what they want, because these are assertive behaviors that are accepted and rewarded in men and often rejected and disliked in women. Women using such assertive behaviors find themselves once again in the double-bind dilemma of being damned if they do assert themselves and doomed if they don't.

It's not about whether or not women reduce their chances of climbing to the top of organizations, because they don't ask for what they want. In my experience of over twenty-five years in organizations, I have certainly observed this to be true and, at the same time, perfectly understandable. The more interesting and revealing question is why do we continue to reward men who assert what they want and penalize women who demonstrate the same behavior?

What is causal?

If the research is correct and there are now experienced and qualified women in the executive pipeline, that women are just as genetically equipped to lead as men, they can be just as committed to their organizations and ambitious for the top jobs, and equally as effective when they get there, what is really causing such low numbers of women making it to the top? If, as I contend, gender role stereotyping and lack of assertive behavior are only part of the picture, what else is going on that creates organizational cultures that prevent, rather than promote, women attaining senior positions?

Chapter Two

The Unwritten Rules

There has been a lot of media coverage of the confusion and lack of understanding about why there are so few women at the top of organizations. As Ilene Lang, President of Catalyst, stated in November 2007, "Women are dizzy, men are dizzy, and we still don't have a simple straightforward answer as to why there just aren't enough women in positions of leadership."[28] To answer this question we need to look at the *unwritten rules* that determine behavior in today's organizations and how they interact to produce leadership norms and expectations that advantage men and disadvantage women.

The origins of the *unwritten rules* are centuries old, but evolved in terms of modern organizational leadership in the 1950s when men were the privileged group with the best-paid jobs. As family bread-winners, they had wives at home who were full-time mothers and homemakers.[29] Where women today have succeeded in becoming senior leaders, it has been by adapting themselves to the norms of behavior dictated by these *unwritten rules*.

These rules aren't explicitly acknowledged in organizations and they are rarely, if ever, talked about in job interviews, but we all know they exist. What is more, they have produced the predominantly male leaders that control our organizations today. Ask yourself how many organizational leaders you know who do not fit the picture created by the unwritten rules below.

The Unwritten Rules of Senior Leadership in Today's Organizations

1. Senior leaders are available anytime and anywhere

This means:
- They are always available. Full-time work is the norm and part-time work is out of the question or career limiting.
- They must be physically present in an office for ten or more hours per day, with little or no flexible working or working from home.
- They must have total geographical mobility. It is career suicide to turn down a promotion because it is undesirable or inconvenient to move.
- They travel extensively as part of their job.

2. Senior leaders have a linear career path

This means:
- They have a continuous employment history with no career breaks.
- They typically make their career breakthrough in their 30's, with rare second chances if they miss the boat.

3. Senior leaders are competitive

This means:
- They are tough, strong and assertive.
- They are typically motivated by money and position.
- They value career and family, but when these values are in conflict, career takes precedence.

4. Senior leaders promote themselves

This means:
- They build relationships with people who can support their career progression.
- They speak confidently about their accomplishments.
- They know what they want and influence others to get it.

The only changes in these *unwritten rules* since the 1950s are that they have become more extreme. The pace of work is faster, deadlines are tighter, scope of responsibility is greater, hours are longer, and there is more travel as organizations become increasingly global.

It is easy to see how these *unwritten rules* interact to favor men and why many women struggle to attain senior leadership positions, or even to stay in those positions once they are achieved. These implicit rules create a structure in which women can rarely succeed to positions of senior leadership if they also take a career break to have children, or work part-time or flexible hours, while their families are young. It is also tough for women to make their thirties the definitive time for career progress when it is also the prime time for raising a family. To compound their difficulties, research also tells us that money and position, although important, are not the primary motivators for most women. In a 2004 study, when asked what motivates them at work, the two top drivers for male executives were career advancement and financial rewards, while the two top drivers for women were relationships at work and delivering a quality product or service to customers.[30]

This is not to say that many men don't also find life challenging within this traditional leadership structure and might like to change it, given the chance. Many men I know struggle with long hours away from their families and excessive travel away from home. But as long as these *unwritten rules* create norms of behavior for senior organizational leaders, the reality remains that women will always be disadvantaged over men. This is particularly true in a world where professional women still take on the bulk of child care and homemaking responsibilities, in addition to their career. It's not that women can't make it to the top within this structure. That has been amply proven by women who have succeeded in positions of senior leadership. But the *unwritten rules* create significant disadvantages and make it considerably more difficult.

Think leader, think male

When we look at the *unwritten rules*, which extend across all sectors, professions, and industries, it is easier to understand why sexual discrimination, prejudice, and gender stereotypes exist. These rules produce norms of behaviors, values, and lifestyle to which our organizational leaders are expected to conform. It is expected that leaders will be assertive and tough enough to make others aware of their strengths and achievements and negotiate strongly for promotion and increased salaries and benefits. They will generally need to make definitive career breakthroughs in their thirties, and although they may have families, they will need to put their jobs first. This will involve being available 24/7 with long hours in an office and a lot of time traveling away from home. It is unlikely that they will have taken any kind of career break or ever worked flexible hours or part-time. These are not the only requirements of leaders in today's organizations, but they are the ones that significantly impact women by creating a structure in which it is extremely difficult to be a woman and to be a senior leader. There might be exceptions to these norms, but they are still true for most people in most organizations.

When we look at these elements it makes sense that women receive fewer senior leadership opportunities than men, even with equivalent qualifications and abilities, because they clearly don't fit the norms of behaviors, values, and lifestyle that the *unwritten rules* require. Women who succeed to the top of organizations do so by recognizing and understanding these rules and adapting their lives and their behaviors to fit them. They must be assertive enough to promote themselves and tough enough to negotiate for what they want; they must choose not to have children, or return to work within a very short time of giving birth; they must allow others to be primary caregivers to their families, because they will spend most of their waking hours at the office, traveling and networking; and they must be resilient enough to weather the personal attacks that originate from their lack of conformity to female stereotypes. It is this last element that often takes the biggest toll.

In her autobiography, Carly Fiorina (CEO of Hewlett Packard 1999-2005) says: "I've never thought of myself as a woman in business. I've thought of myself as a person doing business who happens to be a woman."[31] She goes on to say:

"When I finally reached the top, after striving my entire career to be judged by results and accomplishments, the coverage of my gender, my appearance and the perceptions of my personality would vastly outweigh anything else ... It is undeniable that the words spoken and written about me made my life and my job infinitely more difficult."[32]

In her 2008 bid for the Democratic presidential nomination, Hillary Clinton faced very different treatment from Barack Obama, her male Democratic rival. The media reported:

"Her laugh is a 'cackle.' Her daughter, Chelsea, is being 'pimped out.' She is only there because of her husband. She is 'inauthentic' and manipulative, especially that time she cried in New Hampshire ... When Ms. Clinton wasn't very occasionally showing her soft side, she was characterized as grating and aggressive. When she demonstrated how much she knew about so many issues, she was trying too hard to be 'the smartest girl in the room'... MSNBC's Chris Matthews even called Ms. Clinton an 'uppity woman.' Imagine any commentator calling Mr. Obama an 'uppity black' and keeping his job."[33]

Senior women leaders are an exception to the rule and, as such, are often perceived as either going against the norms of leadership or against the norms of femininity. This creates the double-bind dilemma mentioned in Chapter One. Those women who conform to the behavioral norms dictated by the *unwritten rules* are often disliked for being too assertive, too selfish, too self-promoting, and too competitive. On the other hand, if they conform to the traditional feminine stereotype of being warm, caring, selfless, modest, and responsive, they are generally liked, but not seen as good leadership material. As Hillary Clinton stated in a *New Yorker* interview: "I think that the world is only beginning to recognize that women should be permitted the same range of leadership styles that we permit men."[34]

The *unwritten rules* are firmly entrenched in our organizations and show little sign of changing. This is not a male conspiracy to keep women out of positions of power. Men do not get up in the morning thinking, "How can I keep women down today?"—at least not any men I know. These leadership norms have evolved and become more extreme over time. And we have to ask ourselves, what would motivate men (because they are the ones with most of the power in this situation) to change the well-established, *unwritten rules* of organizational leadership that in their view do the job they are meant to do and offer them every advantage? The current approach used by those trying to motivate change in this arena is to present a good business case for more senior women leaders.

The business case for change

For many years, people (mainly women) have been valiantly trying to motivate change that would create a fairer and more hospitable climate in organizations for women who aspire to lead. They have produced strong arguments about the benefits of having more women on boards and executive teams. The business case for more senior women leaders rests on three key claims: firstly, an increase in women at the top may produce better financial performance for the organization; secondly, more diverse top teams produce better team dynamics and less "group think"; and thirdly, in the "war for talent," there is a pool of underutilized women ready to step forward and help fill the void.

Financial performance

One of the strongest arguments advanced by advocates of increasing the representation of women at the top of organizations is a link between the number of women board directors and women corporate officers and the financial performance of an organization. Catalyst research on the benefits of more women on corporate boards and in corporate officer ranks reported "companies with higher percentages of women board directors, on average, financially outperformed companies with the lowest percentages of women board directors by significant margins. The same correlation exists between the percentage of women corporate officers and financial performance."[35] They also report, however, that the number of women gaining access to this elite level of corporate leadership has now stalled.[36] This is significant not only because of the link between women and financial performance, but also because the additional correlation found that "women board directors are a predictor of women corporate officers: the more women board directors a company has in the past, the more women corporate officers it will have in the future."[37] Therefore, if the number of women at the top of organizations is not growing significantly it is likely to adversely impact the number of women on executive teams.

Similar research in 2004 in the United Kingdom reported that over the previous three years, of the one hundred companies studied, the sixty-nine companies with women directors had recorded an average return on equity (ROE) of 13.8 percent, compared to an average ROE of only 9.9 percent for the thirty-one companies that had all-male boards.[38] The results of both the U.K. and U.S. studies are statistically significant. They do not, however, prove a causal link between women at the top of corporations and increased financial performance. The authors of the Catalyst report point out that the relationship could be "causative," or it could be "spurious" and related to other variables. The studies therefore put forward a strong hypothesis that companies with women on boards outperform those with all-male boards, but they do not prove causality.

More recently, research published in 2009 from Michel Ferrary, professor of Human Resources at CERAM Business School in France, shows that companies with a higher ratio of women in management have better resisted the current global financial crisis. Using data from organizations in the CAC40 (equivalent to the FTSE 100 and Dow Jones), Professor Ferrary demonstrates that "the fewer women a company has in its management, the greater the drop in its share price since the beginning of the year; and the more women in management, the smaller the drop in share price."[39] Ferrary concludes with two questions: Does having more female managers lead to better business performance? Or, does more gender diversity in management equal better business performance? Either way, his research adds to the growing data that supports the business case for more women in positions of real influence inside today's organizations.

Extending the research from financial performance to a wider corporate performance, McKinsey, a global management-consulting firm, has carried out extensive work on the relationship between organizational and financial performance and on the number of women who are managers. Their research has shown that "the companies around the world with the highest scores on nine important dimensions of organization—from leadership and direction to accountability and motivation—are likely to have higher operating margins than their lower-ranked counterparts ... those with three or more women on their senior-management teams scored higher on all nine organizational criteria than did companies with no senior-level women."[40] Once again, this research does not show a causal relationship between women in senior positions and corporate performance, but the authors do claim that their research argues for "greater gender diversity among corporate leaders." Their argument is further supported by work done at the business schools of Columbia University and the University of Maryland. Using data on fifteen hundred U.S. companies from 1992 to 2006, the authors concluded "at least indicative evidence that greater female representation in senior-management positions leads to—and is not merely a result of—better firm quality and performance."[41]

Gender diversity and group dynamics

Further support for more women at the top of organizations comes in the form of the change in group dynamics that women bring to previously all-male boards. Research carried out in conjunction with the Wellesley Centers for Women in Wellesley, Massachusetts, indicates "dramatic differences among boards with one, two, or at least three women directors." After interviewing fifty women directors, twelve CEOs (nine of them male), and seven corporate secretaries (one of them male) at Fortune 1000 companies, the report concluded that women directors make three contributions that men are less likely to make: "They broaden boards' discussions to better represent the concerns of a wide set of stakeholders, including employees, customers, and the community at large. They can be more dogged than men in pursuing answers to difficult questions…and they tend to bring a more collaborative approach to leadership, which improves communication among directors and between the board and management."[42] The report also highlights that in order to reap the benefits of these contributions, boards need to have three or more women. "At that critical mass, our research shows, women tend to be regarded by other board members not as 'female directors' but simply as directors, and they don't report being isolated or ignored … In 2005, only 76 of the Fortune 500 had three or more women on their boards."[43]

The 2009 Ernst & Young report, *Groundbreakers: Using the strength of women to rebuild the world economy*,[44] brings together research that makes a clear case for more diversity at the top of organizations and more women leaders in business. Having more women leaders, they claim, is one way to reform the kind of corporate 'groupthink' culture that has contributed to the current economic crisis. In the report, Lou Pagnutti, Ernst & Young CEO, states: "Investing in women to drive economic growth is not simply about morality or fairness. It's about honing a competitive edge … Diversity is not a 'nice to have.' It's a business imperative." The report concludes that increasing the numbers of women leaders won't happen by accident and recommends that companies plan for it and put mentoring programs in place to ensure the advancement of women.

War for talent

In 1997 and 2000 McKinsey conducted studies on the "War for Talent," drawing attention to an imminent shortage of executives.[45] Today they maintain that "the problem remains acute—and if anything has become worse."[46] Finding talent is, apparently, one of the most important issues keeping business leaders awake at night. A 2006 McKinsey global survey indicated that "the respondents regarded finding talented people as likely to be the single most important managerial preoccupation for the rest of this decade." A second study conducted in 2007 revealed that "nearly half of the respondents expect intensifying competition for talent—and the increasingly global nature of that competition—to have a major effect on their companies over the next five years. No other global trend was considered nearly as significant."[47] This study, of course, was completed before the current global economic crisis which, I suspect, has now become the number one issue keeping business leaders awake at night. However, the war for talent has not gone away and will still be there when the economy recovers.

The talent shortages in many countries and regions have been getting worse. In the United States the imminent retirement of the baby boomers is likely to result in losing large numbers of senior level executives in a short period of time; nearly one-fifth of the working-age population (sixteen and older) will be at least sixty-five by 2016.[48] In Europe, it is estimated that by 2040 there will be a shortfall of twenty-four million workers aged fifteen to sixty-five; raising the proportion of women in the workplace to that of men would reduce the gap to three million.[49]

Advocates of increasing the representation of women in middle and senior management see this issue as part of the business case for women. Recruiting, retaining, and advancing women should help organizations battle the "war for talent." A 2004 Catalyst report concludes, "Employers that focus on diversity will be positioned better to tap into an increasingly educated and skilled segment of the talent pool."[50] Given that McKinsey's first study highlighted this serious problem over ten years ago, it seems so far to have had little impact on the numbers of women achieving senior management positions.

The case for change

Concentrating on the business case for more women in senior leadership positions is an intelligent approach to trying to bring about change. It is an attempt to motivate those who currently hold power (i.e., male corporate executives, board members, and shareholders), by appealing to their primary need of achieving maximum profit. It's not that there isn't a moral or ethical case for equal access for women; it's simply that the business case is deemed more likely to influence change. As we have seen, however, even with the growing strength of this business case, women are making only very slow progress to the top of organizations and that progress may even be stalling.[51] It is also the case that most of the change effort is directed at enabling women to succeed *within* the structure created by the *unwritten rules* of organizational leadership, rather than exposing and changing the *unwritten rules* themselves. This raises obvious questions: what specifically do women want to change—do they want equal access within the existing structure, or do they want a different structure based on a different set of rules? Who are the real influence targets holding the power and what would motivate them to effect change on a level that would make a significant difference to women and their organizations? What is the likelihood and timescale of change and what choices does this leave women who aspire to senior leadership positions right now?

Chapter Three

Changing the Rules

Given that the *unwritten rules* do not create a level playing field for men and women who aspire to lead, it makes sense that those who are disadvantaged want to change them; hence, many change efforts are currently under way that attempt to do this. There are diversity initiatives that attempt to educate about the value of a diverse workforce and a diverse leadership. There are recruitment and retention initiatives that look at how to create fairer practices in attracting and retaining women, including women returning to the workforce after a career break. There are talent management systems that attempt to identify potential female leaders and nurture them through the system. And there is much talk, but relatively little action, about flexible working hours and career breaks for both men and women. All of these initiatives are valuable and sometimes manage to chip away at some of the *unwritten rules* in some organizations. But bringing about fundamental and sustainable change in creating organizational cultures that would level the playing field for men and women is likely to take much more.

The change equation

There is undoubtedly resistance to exposing the *unwritten rules* of organizational leadership and changing them to something fundamentally different that would eliminate the disparities between men and women. To overcome this resistance, three factors would need to be in place:

1. Those who have the power to effect change need to feel enough dissatisfaction with the current leadership norms to motivate action toward something different. If people aren't dissatisfied enough with the way things are, they are unlikely to make the effort to change to something new.

2. There needs to be a compelling vision of a different leadership model with a different set of rules and norms of behavior that would work better than the existing model, particularly for those who currently hold the power in organizations.

3. There need to be clear first steps on how to get from where women are now to where they want to be, once there is sufficient dissatisfaction and a compelling vision for change.

Expressed in a different way:

Change needs (dissatisfaction x vision x steps) to overcome resistance to change[52]
(This is a useful formula to use in any change situation, not just women and leadership).

Influence targets

In addition to having sufficient dissatisfaction, having the vision, and taking the first steps to bring about change, we also need to be clear on who are the influence targets. In other words, who has the power to change the *unwritten rules* and what would motivate them to do so? The power in organizations sits with the board, the senior executives and, if it is a publicly quoted company, with the shareholders. As we have already seen in chapters one and two, most board and executive positions are held by men. We would have to look at individual organizations to assess the composition of male and female shareholders, but it is safe to say that in big organizations, large proportions of shares are held by investment funds (predominantly managed by men); in smaller companies, individual shareholders are often men with a smaller proportion of women. Other types of organizations such as government, law firms, and academic institutions are, as we have already seen, most often run by men.

All of this to say that, if the *unwritten rules* are to be changed, we can safely assume that the people to be influenced are predominantly men. So the picture we have is of women who are disadvantaged by the current set of rules, trying to influence men who are advantaged by these same rules, to make changes that would allow for a more equal distribution of power at the top of organizations. A 2009 Catalyst study looking at why some men support gender diversity in leadership while others do not, identified the "zero-sum" mentality of many men—a belief that gains for women necessarily mean losses for men.[53] In the same Catalyst report, men who were identified as champions of gender diversity indicated barriers that deter other men from becoming advocates of equality. These barriers to men's support included: fear of losing status, or of being seen as part of the problem, and apathy—a sense that issues of gender do not concern men. We would, therefore, have to conclude that the odds are heavily stacked against women in this situation. When we look at the reality of this picture, the obvious question is, what would motivate men who currently hold positional power in organizations to make changes to a set of *unwritten rules* that would reduce some of their advantage and redistribute it to include more women?

Dissatisfaction

Presenting the business case for more female leaders (Chapter Two) is an attempt to raise dissatisfaction in board members, senior executives and shareholders. If there is a causal relationship, or even a strong case, that more female leaders can result in improved organizational performance and positively impact the bottom line, the officers of the company are duty bound to take action toward appointing more women at the top. This is particularly the case in for-profit organizations where law dictates that corporate officers have a legal duty to shareholders to maximize profit.

"(T)he corporate design contained in hundreds of corporate laws throughout the world is nearly identical...the people who run corporations have a legal duty to shareholders, and that duty is to make money. Failing this duty can leave directors and officers open to being sued by shareholders."[54]

If a causal link could be proved between more senior women at the top and improved organizational performance leading to increased profit, it might be possible to create sufficient dissatisfaction among shareholders that they would apply pressure on the predominantly all-male boards to appoint more women. As we have seen, research is already indicating a strong hypothesis, if not an actual causal relationship. Getting more women on boards does not, however, change the *unwritten rules* or the behavioral norms that they produce. It simply allows more women to succeed within the current rules.

If the legal mandate of for-profit organizations is to make as much money for shareholders as is legally possible, this in itself could be a force in play against any change in the *unwritten rules*. Having intelligent, highly skilled corporate officers working eighty-plus-hour weeks in the pursuit of more profit aligns very well with the legal mandate of for-profit organizations. As long as there is a steady supply of people—men and women—willing to work in this way, there is unlikely to be sufficient dissatisfaction to change the way leaders are expected to behave and live their lives.

In terms of actively promoting more women to the top now or in the short term, there is no evidence of sufficient dissatisfaction to bring about change—not by promoting more women within the current context and certainly not by confronting and changing the *unwritten rules* themselves. It is unrealistic to expect men who currently hold senior positions in organizations to feel dissatisfied with either the system that helped get them where they are or in the situation of inequity for women. If those wanting change recognize the need to raise dissatisfaction, their best course of action would be to focus on shareholders and governments. Shareholders can put pressure on boards to promote more women, if they think it will benefit the bottom line, and governments can change the law to get greater representation of women at the top of organizations, as they have done in Scandinavia.[55]

Compelling vision

To influence change we also need a clear enough picture of where we are now (current reality) and where we want to be (end result). Dissatisfaction with the small number of women at the top of organizations is not enough. There needs to be a compelling vision of how more women in positions of power in organizations will somehow be better than what we have now. In current attempts to influence this, what is often unclear is whether women and their male advocates want to *change* the *unwritten rules* that govern leadership behavior, or whether they want equal opportunity and access *within* the context of these rules. Being clear about specifically what we are trying to influence is essential to actually getting it. If we wanted to be radical and change the rules, rather than have women continue to try to adapt to them, what would a compelling vision look like?

The Scandinavian model

Imagine a workplace where consensus is more highly valued than hierarchy and self-promotion, where parental leave is considered an important component of professional development, where the wage gap between men and women is considered an urgent problem and is being solved with government support, where the lives of employees are valued both within the workplace and without, and where salaries are less important than quality of life. Imagine a business culture where family is considered important enough to include more vacation time, one-year maternity leave on full pay and six weeks "papa leave," and where the workday is constructed around when mothers and fathers need to be home, because there is a strong value that both parents need to be involved in parenting. And imagine a society where expanded child care and parental insurance make it easy for both parents to work. This utopian picture is not a fantasy; it is alive and well in Scandinavia.

Inger Buus, a researcher at the Danish Institute, describes the cornerstones of Scandinavian leadership as

> "respect for the individual; a humanistic and value-based approach that would include the public, private and voluntary sectors, as well as activist movements, trade unions and employee representatives; non-bureaucratic organizations with a high degree of devolved responsibility and accountability to create empowering and enabling environments that stimulate creativity, innovation, and collaboration; finally, trust, care and concern as key values."[56]

It's no accident that there are considerably higher numbers of women on boards in Scandinavian countries. In 2002 Norway introduced legislation that targeted 40 percent female board members by 1 January 2008. A European Professional Women's Network 2008 survey reported that Norway now has 44.2 percent of women on boards (up from 22 percent in 2004), Sweden posted 26.9 percent (up from 22.8 percent in 2006), whereas Finland and Denmark recorded 25.7 percent and 18.1 percent, respectively (up from 20 percent and 17.9 percent). All Scandinavian countries continue to outperform the rest of Europe in this area.

> "In Norway, Sweden and Finland, the average number of women on boards has passed the significant number of three, signaling that these countries have clearly moved away from tokenism and are convinced of the positive impact on their results gender diversity brings."[57]

This European movement seems to be spreading. In 2007 Spain adopted a special provision in their Equality Act, enforcing companies to have at least 40 percent women on their boards in eight years' time. In Germany, Chancellor Angela Merkel's government is heading in the same direction, with an initial step of a "voluntary charter" committed to gender equality, and the Netherlands is committing to putting more women in charge at the top.

Envisioning a different set of guiding rules and a different model that would fundamentally change women's access to senior leadership positions isn't difficult. Realizing it—in macho, male-dominated, competitive cultures—obviously isn't easy. Those who want to change the *unwritten rules* of organizational leadership can draw hope from the fact that in 2002 of Norway's 611 leading companies, 470 had no female board members and little more than 6 percent of all board positions were occupied by women. Two key factors brought about the dramatic change: firstly, the change initiative was led by a powerful man, Ansgar Gabrielsen, the minister for trade and industry at the time (2001-2004), who introduced the legislation that targeted 40 percent female board members by 1 January 2008. In an interview with the U.K. *Sunday Times* in 2008 he stated, "Sometimes you have to create an earthquake, a tsunami, to get things to change ...If a left-wing feminist had come out with something like that it would have been dismissed as just another scream in the night ... But because I said it, I knew that people would take notice."[58] Gabrielsen was not motivated by creating equality between the sexes; his boardroom revolution was inspired by U.S. studies (Chapter Two) showing a strong link between more women at the top of organizations and increased organizational and financial performance.

The second decisive factor was public mood and opinion. Although Norwegian business leaders (the men with the power) threw their toys out of the cot, warning of dire consequences: "a decrease in company competence, plunging shareholder confidence and a flight of foreign capital"—in other words, "the prospect of high heels kicking the chairs from under the men who dominated boardrooms would create economic meltdown,"[59]—the general public passionately embraced the plan. Gabrielsen had his finger on Norway's pulse and the coalition government and corporate executives had no choice but to back his proposals.

Today it is too early to assess the real impact on the bottom line of Norwegian companies, but signs are promising. A survey of the colleagues of women newly appointed to Norwegian board positions "showed that most of them have significantly higher educational and professional qualifications than many of the male colleagues they replaced, or sit next to. The women are not only brighter, they are younger, and the majority have distinguished themselves in a wide variety of other professional careers before being appointed to company boards."[60] There is clearly no shortage of women in the executive pipeline willing to work in Norway.

In a recent interview, Gabrielsen gleefully hammered home his views, saying:

"What's the point in pouring a fortune into educating girls, and then watching them exceed boys at almost every level, if, when it comes to appointing business leaders in top companies, these are drawn from just half the population—friends who have been recruited on fishing and hunting trips or from within a small circle of acquaintances … It's all about tapping into valuable under-utilised resources."[61]

In a July 2009 *Fast Company* article, *"Norway's Boards: Two Years Later, What Difference Do Women Make?"* a number of board members were interviewed to give a *"so what"* on the legislation two years after it's introduction. The ratio of interviews was 50 percent men and 50 percent women and almost all of the interviewees had originally objected to the 40 percent female board quota.

"Two years later, in a series of one-on-one interviews, every single person said that the boards were measurably improved with the addition of the women. A couple of the boards already had a lot of women: those folks tended to think that a legislation solution had not been necessary. But those who experienced the resistance to having women on boards and then lived the difference when the issue was forced supported the legislation. The reason: the change would never have happened unless it was required."[62]

There is no doubt in my mind that to create an environment in which women can be true to their values, behave authentically as women, and lead organizations, the *unwritten rules* would need to evolve in a way that reflects the values underpinning what is being achieved in Scandinavia. There is no evidence, however, of any appetite for this level of change in North America and other parts of Europe, although some think the current economic climate might motivate enough dissatisfaction for some level of change, perhaps creating an opportunity for women. In Europe, it will be interesting to see if other countries start to implement changes that allow the current leadership model and the *unwritten rules* themselves to evolve, as in Scandinavia, or if they take the route of implementing measures that enable greater access for women *within* the constraints of the existing *unwritten rules*. It is often considered easier to make change within an existing structure, than to radically change the structure itself.

Succeeding within the context of the unwritten rules

Indications are that, if it is to become the norm that more women lead organizations, governments, and countries, it is likely, in the short term, to happen *within* the existing set of rules, as opposed to fundamentally changing the rules themselves. Even within this existing structure, significant increases in women succeeding to positions of senior leadership are not likely to happen anytime soon without influencing shareholders and governments to take action. These are the two groups that have the most power to overcome the natural resistance to change that exists at the top of most organizations. If shareholders are made aware and believe evidence that links increased organizational performance with more gender diversity at the top there is a chance that they will start to insist on change. The other route is for governments to implement quotas for the number of women on boards, as is happening in some European countries.

Quotas and reverse discrimination

Implementing mandatory quotas for the number of women on boards is a form of reverse discrimination, "the practice of favoring a historically disadvantaged group at the expense of members of a historically advantaged group. The term 'reverse discrimination' reflects the fact that the group now being discriminated against had previously been the one doing the discriminating."[63] Many argue that, by introducing quotas for women at the top of organizations, we would simply be replacing one form of discrimination with another.

There is considerable resistance to proceeding along this route, not least from some women. The idea that women might be promoted based on their gender rather than their ability to do the job is offensive to many. "There is no appetite for quotas here," commented Jacey Graham, co-director of a FTSE-100 cross-company mentoring program for women and the author of a recently published book on women in boardrooms in the United Kingdom.[64] "There is an appetite to facilitate talented women coming through, but they must be seen to compete on the same terms as male colleagues."[65]

When the leader of the British Conservative Party, David Cameron, suggested that he would implement a quota of women cabinet ministers to address gender imbalance in government, some of his most outspoken opposition came from his female colleagues. The former Conservative minister, Anne Widdecombe, said she would be "grossly insulted" if she were given a front-bench position on those terms.[66]

Other women have pushed their opposition even further. Anna Dugdale, board director and one of the few female financial advisers to a large British National Health Service teaching trust is on record as saying, "I think a quota law would be the worst thing possible for women. You would never know if you were there on your own merit or owing to some legal requirement."[67] Women might want support for equal access to positions of power, but many do not want the type of support that could undermine their credibility.

But let's take another look at Norway where the quota system for women on boards is actually in operation. To remind ourselves, despite massive opposition to quota legislation when it was first introduced in 2002, as of June 2008 Norway had 44.2 percent of women on boards, up from 22 percent in 2004. The Confederation of Norwegian Enterprise (NHO), one of Norway's most traditional and conservative organizations, was one of the institutions vehemently opposed to quotas from the outset:

"As an employer's organization, although we wanted more women in senior positions, we were against the quota law from day one, believing such decisions were entirely up to shareholders," said Sigrun Vageng, an executive director of the NHO. "We thought that the threat of closing companies if they did not comply was quite ridiculous. But now we have to acknowledge that it is only because of the law and the public debate it provoked that real change has happened."[68]

Kjell Erik Oie, Norway's state secretary for equality and children has also said, "There's no going back ...We've realised it's good for business."[69]

The reality in Norway today is that quota legislation for women on boards has succeeded where all other efforts had failed. So much so that the debate on the rights and wrongs of the quota system has become a thing of the past—they are too busy getting on with it and making it work for the benefit of business. I would encourage those who are working hard to level the playing field for women to take notice of this reality, rather than be deterred by the voices of those opposed to change through quota legislation on the basis that it undermines women's credibility. It's not that the naysayers don't have a good point. Of course women would rather be promoted on their ability than as part of a quota system. Reality is, however, that this is unlikely to happen within the current context of the *unwritten rules*, evidenced by the slow progression of women onto boards and the fact that this movement might even be stalling.[70] Just as it took a change in legislation to give women the vote at the beginning of the twentieth century, so it may take similar action at the beginning of the twenty-first century to overcome the resistance to women leading organizations, governments, and countries.

Influencing governments to change legislation and influencing shareholders to pressure their boards requires coordinated effort by groups that hold some kind of influence or power. You might like to start or join such a group if you feel passionate enough about bringing about change.

Current reality is that outside of Scandinavia there appears to be little appetite to change the *unwritten rules* that create the norms of leadership and organizational behavior anytime in the near future. And so where does this leave you right now if you are a woman aspiring to lead within the context of these *rules*? Given that we can't all move to Norway, what choices do you have about your career path? What can you do to support yourself if leading in today's organizations is part of your career and life aspirations?

Section Two of this book speaks to women who understand the challenges of succeeding with the structure created by the *unwritten rules* and who still choose to tread this path. If you are one of these women, the next section will help you to make informed choices about if, when, and where to lead in today's organizations. It will also provide essential professional development that will dramatically increase your chances of achieving your career ambitions.

Section Two
What Does a Woman Need to Do to Get on Around Here?

INTRODUCTION

It's difficult to make good choices without all of the relevant information. The purpose of Section One was to provide more information and context about the organizational environment that women must understand and navigate if they are to achieve positions of senior leadership. Greater understanding usually provokes more thought and, in this case, hopefully, more informed decisions about how to move forward and create the life and the career that you want.

If, after reading Section One, you still aspire to senior leadership within today's organizations, this section will help you think carefully and be more fully in touch with the reality of what you are signing up for. The *unwritten rules* dictate that, if you are a woman in your thirties who does not intend to have children; who wants to devote her life to her job; who enjoys working in different parts of the world; who is motivated by money and position; who can be tough, strong and assertive; who can build good networks and negotiate for what she wants; and who is able to bounce back from the inevitable attacks on your femininity; then you are an ideal candidate for senior leadership in today's organizations. If you step outside any of these norms created by the *unwritten rules*—which, of course, you almost certainly will—then be aware of what is likely to come your way and be prepared. This picture is not intended to deter you, just to ensure that you are in touch with reality as it currently stands for women in today's organizations and that you are making conscious and informed choices.

Section Two of this book is based on the assumption that the *unwritten rules* are unlikely to change dramatically anytime soon and that if you are a woman who aspires to higher levels of leadership *now* you need to not only understand these *rules*, but know how to develop yourself and behave effectively within them. This section provides essential skill development to support you in your journey toward achieving senior leadership positions and advice on how to stay sane and healthy while you are doing it. Chapters Five through Nine take one or more of the *unwritten rules* and look at what you can do to succeed within the organizational culture that these *rules* create. Chapter Four lays the groundwork for this skill development by outlining the due diligence you should do on your organization and on yourself to ensure that you create the best possible chance of succeeding.

Chapter Four

Due Diligence

Taking control of your career, rather than simply reacting and responding to opportunities and setbacks that come your way, requires conducting due diligence on both yourself and your organization. Due diligence in this context refers to an investigation of your own performance in your current role, your perceived potential to move higher within your company, and a good look at the performance of your organization in supporting and promoting women.

Due diligence on your organization

If you aspire to a senior a leadership position in your company it would make sense to lift your head from your everyday work and look around to make a realistic assessment of your organizational environment to see if it supports your aspirations. In other words, is there any chance of your making it around here? Given what you see around you or what you can find out from talking to others, try to answer as many as possible of the following questions:

- Are there three or more women on your board of directors?

- Are there three or more women on your senior executive team?

- Do you see men and women gaining promotion based on their competence and potential (as opposed to their candidacy for the old boys' club)?

- Are there successful diversity initiatives implemented across the organization sponsored by senior management?

- Are you seeing a steady increase in the numbers of women in middle and senior management?

- Does your company have a talent management system that encourages and supports women in their aspirations for promotion?

- Are there strategies for increasing the visibility of women role models, such as networking events and diversity forums?

- Is there diversity education and awareness building through mandatory manager training?

- Does your company have a variety of work-life programs and policies, including flextime and family leave for women and men?

- Do you have strong accountability mechanisms, such as a global HR scorecard, employee surveys, and the key performance indicators (KPIs), which are linked with managers' targets for promoting and developing women leaders?

- Are metrics, such as the number of women senior managers and high-performer retention rates, as well as career development and overall employee satisfaction scores, closely tracked?

- Does your company have a review process that assesses and tracks the current and future pipeline of women into executive management?

- Do you have any business processes that increase management's familiarity with talented women managers?

- Are there any initiatives that address development, training, and mentoring needs of women?

- Does your company sponsor global programs that bring together potential women clients and the firm's senior women to discuss topics such as governmental affairs, economics, and business?

- Do you have a company-wide women's network with regional chapters that benefits women across the organization?

- Is there a process to ensure transparency and accountability of people development and career advancement?

- Do you have access to your company's leadership strategy and competencies required to advance to senior-level positions?

These are an amalgamation of examples of real initiatives from a mixture of different organizations. The point here is not that you need to check every box to signify that your organization is a good place for women to work, but you should be able to check at least some of these items if your company provides an environment in which you can succeed to higher levels of leadership. Many organizations have not only recognized the value of diversity and the business case for more women in middle and senior leadership roles, they are proactively taking action toward it:

Baxter International Inc., is a global healthcare company with $12.3 billion in sales (2008) and approximately 48, 500 employees. Its subsidiaries assists healthcare professionals and their patients with treatment of complex medical conditions including hemophilia, immune disorders, kidney disease, trauma and other conditions. In 2005 Baxter's Asia Pacific operations developed a talent management initiative that strived to develop a 50/50 gender balance across management-level and critical positions throughout 14 countries in the region. It's goal was achieved two years ahead of plan by delivering solid increases of women in critical positions across its Asia Pacific operations: women in management and executive positions increased from 31 percent in 2004 to 50 percent in 2008 and 4 out of 16 general managers are women. Representation of women in individual countries is also strong: approximately 30 to 70 percent of management and executive positions in each of the 14 respective countries are held by women. From 2006 to 2008, women's representation on the Asia Pacific Leadership Team increased from 25 to 37 percent.

CH2M Hill is a global engineering and construction firm with gross revenues of $5 billion (2007) and approximately 25,000 employees in regional offices worldwide. Their Constructing Pathways for Women Through Inclusion initiative provides a model for leveraging women employees to achieve business success in a traditionally male-dominated industry. They have attempted to create an environment in which diversity, openness, and innovation thrive, which includes regional women's networks that provide local learning and mentoring opportunities; Women's Leadership Summits that deliver strategic learning opportunities to a cross-section of women leaders; informal mentoring and networking opportunities; targeted recruiting for both new graduates and experienced hires; a formal succession-planning process that ensures slates are diverse and include at least one woman or person of color; vigorous recruiting of women and people of color into the firm; and substantial involvement by the Board of Directors Workforce and Diversity Committee in developing strategy and policy. Since the initiative's launch in 2003, women's representation in senior leadership positions has increased from 2.9 percent to 18.0 percent, and women of color lead two of the company's 13 geographic regions. The percentage of women project managers has also increased from 20.5 percent in 2005 to 30.3 percent in 2008.

Scotiabank, a Canadian-based bank with 69,000 employees and 12.5 million customers in 50 countries around the world has significantly improved its representation of women at senior management levels through its Unlocking Potential, Delivering Results: The Advancement of Women Initiative. Two central elements drive the initiative: a process to ensure transparency and accountability of people development and career advancement; and a series of programs that connect and develop women. Their online tool "HR Passport" provides all employees with access to the bank's leadership strategy and competencies required to advance to senior-level positions. Programs such as ScotiaWomen's Connection, a bank-wide women's network, are webcast globally and provide women with visibility and access to senior leaders and role models. Essential to the success of the program are the formal accountability mechanisms and metrics that are in place. Advancement of Women targets and results are included in leaders' individual balanced scorecards and are linked to their overall performance, which is tied to compensation. Through this initiative, Scotiabank has significantly improved its representation of women at the senior management level from 18.9 percent in 2003 to 31.0 percent in 2006. Representation of women at the most senior EVP/corporate officer level has increased from 26.7 percent to 36.8 percent from 2003 to 2006.

[71]All examples from the Catalyst Web site

If, after conducting due diligence on your present organization, you come to the conclusion that you are unlikely to achieve your aspirations where you are, it might be time to look around for a position in a more "woman-friendly" company. A source that might be helpful is the Catalyst Web site (www.catalyst.org). The "Catalyst Award Winners" page describes organizations that have achieved recognition for their focus and efforts on enabling women to succeed (see examples above). In addition it is also easy, thanks to the Internet, to investigate any organization by accessing their Web site and exploring their board and senior management composition to see how well women are represented. For example, as of September 2009, Avon not only had Andrea Jung, a woman CEO, they also had more women in management than any other Fortune 500 company. Five of their eleven board members were women, and six out of their thirteen top-level senior leaders were women. Remember that, as illustrated in Chapter Two, the more women there are on the board, the more likely it is that women will be promoted to senior management in that organization.

Should you decide to explore alternative organizations that you think might provide a more woman-friendly environment ensure that you conduct your due diligence on them before making any move. The list above provides not only essential questions to ask in your current organization, but also provides areas to explore when looking at any prospective new company.

If you ask questions about how serious your organization is in enabling women to succeed to senior positions, you should be able to assess whether or not it is the right place for you to enjoy working and to achieve your career ambitions. This is an important step in your career planning. Why make it even more difficult to succeed by working in an organization that does not recognize the value of diversity and the obstacles that women face in their journey to senior management and at least try to help overcome them? If, for some reason, you are unable or unwilling to leave your current organization, even though the evidence shows that it does not support women in becoming senior leaders, at least be aware that the odds are stacked against you and you are likely to have to work even harder to make it up the career ladder in your current environment.

Due diligence on your own performance

As a woman, to even be in the game and considered as a candidate for promotion, you need to be doing an outstanding job in your current role. As we have seen in Section One, women often need to outperform men to be seen as their equals. Part of your baseline, therefore, is to excel in your current role and to expect that you might sometimes go unrecognized for your success or passed over for a promotion in favor of a man with less impressive performance results. We know that this sometimes happens and we know from the first three chapters of this book why it happens. In such situations you need to persist in proving your competence and redouble your efforts. I know this isn't fair, but it is the reality of the *unwritten rules* and the stereotypes and norms of behavior that they produce. Remember, this is what you signed up for in choosing the journey to senior leadership in today's organizations, so don't get fazed by it. There are actions you can take that will reduce the chance of your being passed over for promotion and support your career advancement, such as expanding your ability to influence and building support and advocacy, but more on this in later chapters. The message here is that being outstanding in your current role is the baseline that enables you to sit at the interview table with men who may or may not have performed as well as you.

Managing your boss

To achieve outstanding performance, it is essential that you and your boss have clear statements and agreements about your success criteria. In other words, establish clear objectives and standards of measurement so that you know exactly how your performance will be assessed and by whom. Do not wait until an annual assessment to discuss how you are doing. Meet with your boss frequently throughout the year to review your performance against objectives. It is up to you to manage this and ensure it happens, even if your boss is difficult to pin down. Women who make it to senior level positions within the context of the *unwritten rules* know that they have to outperform their male colleagues, consistently prove their abilities, and manage their bosses to ensure recognition.

Andrea (not her real name) was a vice president in a large pharmaceutical company. As part of her executive coaching, I conducted feedback interviews with her boss, her boss's boss, her peers and her direct reports. The feedback was outstanding – probably the most glowing feedback report I have ever compiled for a coaching client. Imagine my surprise as I was talking her through the report when her eyes filled with tears and she visibly struggled to continue. I thought that perhaps she was simply overwhelmed by the admiration of her colleagues. Instead, she disclosed that she was, of course, pleased and gratified that she was so well thought of and that she was considered a "high potential" candidate for an even bigger job in the future. The truth, however, was that she was considering leaving the organization and had already started responding to enquiries from other companies. Even though she currently held a large, demanding and high profile position she felt under-stimulated and impatient for the next big move that she had been promised upon joining the organization. It was vital to Andrea to be stretched and challenged and she felt her current role was well within her capability. As part of the coaching, we learned together that she was not managing her boss well to ensure that he knew how she felt, what she needed and when she needed it. He was about to lose one of his star players without really having the chance to save the situation because she was not being clear with him about how she felt.

The outcome of disclosing where she stood and what she needed in a clean and clear way with her boss was that she did achieve the much bigger role that she desired within the timeframe that she had set. The feedback and coaching that she received triggered a chain of events that created a big win for both Andrea and for her organization.

Managing and getting feedback from your boss is part of the continuing due diligence that you need to be conducting on your own performance.

Getting feedback

To get a good picture of how you are perceived in your organization and to hear the truth about your chances of promotion, it is essential to get honest feedback. Don't rely solely on annual assessments from your manager as your only source of understanding how you are doing. I have coached many people, women and men, who have received consistently good annual reviews and who still don't get the promotions they want and don't really know why. There are various ways that you can get feedback as part of your due diligence on your own performance.

If you have a talent management system in your organization, you must get yourself in the top tier and be considered a "high potential," if you are serious about ascending to a senior management position. If you are already a high potential (or whatever terminology your company uses) and have been identified for promotion in the short term, your job is to keep up the good work and be as clear as you can about what it is you want to do next. Even if you have not identified a specific role in the organization that you want, at the very least you need to have identified what type of role you aspire to, for example it might be something like "an operations role managing complex demands and large groups of people, preferably in North America or Europe." You also need to identify who sits on your talent management board because these are the people who will have a significant say in either supporting or resisting your next move. When you have identified these people, you should ensure that they know who you are, what you are good at, and what it is you aspire to do. Arrange meetings with them, preferably face-to-face or, if that's not possible, by phone, to discuss your career aspirations and to ask them for their support by giving you feedback about how to go about achieving your next move. If you think this is being a little pushy you are right; it is, and it is exactly what you must do to prevent being passed over by someone else who has had the good sense to do exactly this. Being clear about what you want with the people who have the power to influence your career is a basic necessity in achieving your goals.

If you are currently not in the top tier of your company's talent management system, you need to take a different approach. Your job then is to find out specifically what you need to do to move from how you are currently perceived to become a high-potential candidate ready for promotion. Again, identify the decision makers and meet with them to inform them of your aspirations and ask for feedback on what you would need to start doing, stop doing or do differently for them to consider you a high potential candidate. Some people are not experienced in giving feedback in a way that is clear and useful. Comments such as "you need to have more presence" or "you need to be more like a leader" are intended to be helpful, but aren't because you have no idea what you would need to do to have more "presence" or to be "more like a leader." Manage the feedback you receive by asking for it to be specific and behavioral. In other words, ask questions such as: "If I were to display more presence, what would you see and hear me doing?" "If you were filming me, what would I look like and how would you see me behaving if I were more like a leader?" In this way you can help people give you specific behavioral feedback that you can act upon.

There are other methods of getting feedback that can contribute to the due diligence on your own performance. One of the most robust methods is to influence your organization to support your development by hiring an executive coach. Most good coaches will conduct a feedback interview process with your key stakeholders as part of the objective setting for your development. The advantage of having an outside party, such as a coach, conducting the feedback is that he or she will not only have the skill to question your colleagues in such a way that enables really good behavioral feedback, but the feedback is likely to be more candid if your colleagues are talking to a third party. If coaching is not an option for you it is possible to conduct your own feedback process. Most organizations now have a 360-degree feedback tool that can be administered online. Before using this option, check that the questions asked will give you the type of feedback you are after. For example, if you want to get feedback on your competency as a leader, ensure that the questions align with the level of leadership you aspire to and that the questions reflect the real leadership competencies of your organization.

An alternative would be to create a simple feedback tool for your own use. This is much easier than it sounds.

Step 1

Create a key stakeholder web

The purpose of this web is to think about and identify people who can either influence your career progression because of their positions in the organization or who you trust to give you helpful and candid feedback (or both). Put yourself in the center of the web and then think broadly about whom you could approach for helpful feedback. You certainly need to include your boss and probably your boss's boss. Other options might be your HR partner, certain colleagues, a good friend who knows you well, some of your direct reports, and so on.

Example

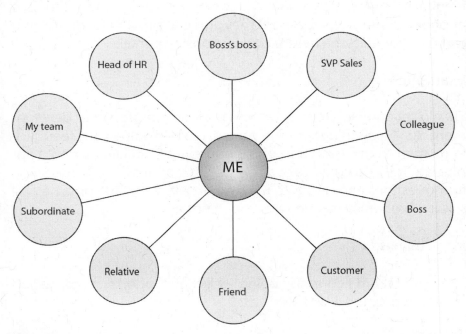

Step 2

Write down a clear and concise statement of the purpose of the feedback. For example: "The purpose of the feedback is to gain a clear understanding of how I need to develop to be a strong candidate for VP Sales in twelve months' time."

Step 3

In relation to the purpose of the feedback, what questions do you want to ask the people on your relationship web? I strongly recommend that you ask a small number of open questions, for example: "What am I currently doing well that you think I should keep doing if

I am to become VP of Sales?" "What should I start doing that would support my becoming VP of Sales?" "What should I stop doing that might prevent my becoming VP of Sales?"

Step 4

Contact your identified key stakeholders to ask for their support and feedback. The more personal you can be the better, so face-to-face or phone contact works best. If they agree to provide feedback, you can then forward the feedback questions by e-mail.

Example:

Thanks for agreeing to support my continuing professional development. As we discussed on the phone, I would value your feedback in relation to my aspiration of becoming a VP of Sales. I would appreciate it if you could take a few minutes to answer the following four questions and return to me by (date). It would be most helpful if you were totally candid with your feedback.

Many thanks.

1. What am I currently doing well that supports my aspiration to become a VP Sales?

2. What should I start doing that I am not currently doing, if I am to become a VP of Sales?

3. What should I stop doing that might prevent me becoming a VP of Sales?

4. Any other helpful comments that you would like to add.

These are some suggestions about how you might conduct due diligence on your current performance and standing within your organization. They are not your only options. You might, for example, simply arrange informal conversations with key stakeholders to talk about your career aspirations and to ask for feedback. I encourage you to think about what works best for you given your current position in your company and your organizational culture in light of what it is you want to achieve. No matter how you do it, the important message is that if you are serious about managing your career, due diligence on both your organization and your current perceived performance (how other key stakeholders see your performance as well as how you see yourself) is essential. It's about being proactive and taking some control of your future, rather than waiting and hoping that you will be recognized and rewarded for a job well done.

Chapter Five

Strategic Influencing Skills

UNWRITTEN RULES:
Senior leaders promote themselves
This means:
- They build relationships with people who can support their career progression.
- They speak confidently about their accomplishments.
- They know what they want and influence others to get it.

Senior leaders are competitive
This means:
- They are tough, strong and assertive.

In Chapter One we identified the double-bind dilemma for women. Women leaders, it seems, can be competent or likable, but rarely both. "When women behave assertively, they tend to be seen as competent, but not as effective interpersonally as women who adopt a more stereotypically feminine style."[72] Somehow women need to navigate the terrain of being assertive enough to be taken seriously as leaders and at the same time being responsive enough to be sufficiently liked and respected that people want to follow them. The ability to work effectively with other people to get things done in a way that maintains or builds good relationships is a key skill for any leader, particularly in today's matrix organizational environments where influence is often more important than positional power. In addition, the ability to use a full range of influencing behaviors is essential for women leaders working within today's organizations because of the double-bind dilemma created by gender stereotyping. In other words, because the stereotypes of traditional leadership and femininity are in conflict, women need to be even more skilled interpersonally to cope with the contradictory expectations of being a leader and being a woman.

Is influence a dirty word?

In my experience of training and coaching hundreds of people to expand their repertoire of influencing skills, it has become evident that the first step for many women is to understand what influence is and how it can be used positively. To some, influence is a dirty word. It is associated with hidden, manipulative techniques to get one's own way at the expense of others. Typical dictionary definitions describe influence in one of two ways: either to *manage or utilize skillfully* or to *control or play upon by artful, unfair, or insidious means especially to one's own advantage.*

The first thing to understand about the behavioral skills of influencing is that they can be used positively or negatively—to *manage or utilize skillfully* or to *control or play upon by artful, unfair, or insidious means.* The skills that I will introduce you to in this chapter are, in themselves, neutral. This means that they can be used negatively to do harm or positively to do well. The intention here is to explore how women can increase their abilities to be positively influential as leaders within the context of the *unwritten rules* of leadership in today's organizations. To this end, the definition of influence we will use here is **to get things done with others while maintaining or building positive working relationships.**

Expanding your repertoire of positive influencing skills

Developing a wider range of behavioral skills and being strategic about how you use them will help you to walk the fine line between being an assertive, credible leader and being a woman who also has the capacity to understand and respond to the needs of others. You can be a leader only if you have people who are willing to follow you. As a leader, if you overuse assertive behaviors and underuse responsive behaviors you will be perceived as aggressive and a "bully broad." If you overuse responsive behaviors and underuse assertive behaviors, you will be perceived as nice, but somewhat passive—particularly within the context of a leadership model that values assertiveness. The real skill is to develop your ability to flex your behavior appropriately to the situation to achieve your objectives with others, rather than achieving your objectives at the expense of others. Developing understanding and skill in eight key influence behaviors will help you to do this. I am indebted to Sheppard Moscow (www.sheppardmoscow.com) for permission to feature this influence model.

A framework for understanding influence

A helpful way to think about influence is to look at the choices we have about how we use our energy when we are interacting with others. Essentially we can use our energy to **push** to achieve our **own agenda** using **positive assertive behaviors** or we can **pull** others toward us and explore **their agendas** by being **positively responsive** (figure 1). When we are using **push energy**, we are trying to influence others by pushing our ideas, views, opinions, expectations, and feelings in order to be clear with others about what we want to happen. When we are using **pull energy**, we are influencing by being responsive and pulling others toward us by listening, exploring others' views, disclosing helpful information, and identifying what we have in common.

We all tend to favor one side of this model. You will know if you generally gravitate toward being clear and assertive about what you want, or if you prefer to listen and respond to what others have to say. In influence situations where we feel comfortable, we can usually work both sides of the model, appropriately asserting our own needs and responding to the needs of others to get good desired end results. In more difficult situations where we are under some kind of pressure, we tend to revert to the energy that feels most comfortable, which isn't always the most appropriate way to respond to get things done and maintain relationships and our own credibility as good leaders. Under pressure we might, for example, push harder for what we want, unintentionally creating stronger resistance, when it would be more influential to pull others toward us by being responsive. Alternatively, we might stay on others' agendas too long and miss the chance to get our own needs met.

By strengthening the behaviors we are already good at and by expanding the repertoire of behaviors available to us when under pressure, it is possible to influence appropriately using both sides of the model in any given situation. This level of behavioral skill also gives women the best chance they have of working the double bind dilemma—being assertive enough to be taken seriously as a leader and responsive enough that people want to be led by them. Figure 1 illustrates the basic framework of how we can use our energy to either push to achieve our own agenda or pull to explore and understand others' agendas. Figure 2 identifies the eight specific positive influence behaviors that correspond with positive push energy and positive pull energy. I strongly recommend that all leaders strengthen and develop these eight key influence behaviors. Specifically for women leaders, developing the expertise to work across the range of influence behaviors provides the tools necessary to lead within the context of the *unwritten rules*.

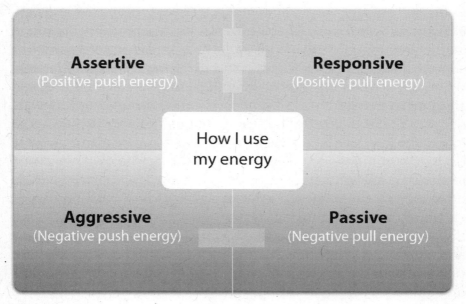

My Agenda   Your Agenda

Assertive   **Responsive**
(Positive push energy)   (Positive pull energy)

How I use
my energy

Aggressive   **Passive**
(Negative push energy)   (Negative pull energy)

Figure 1

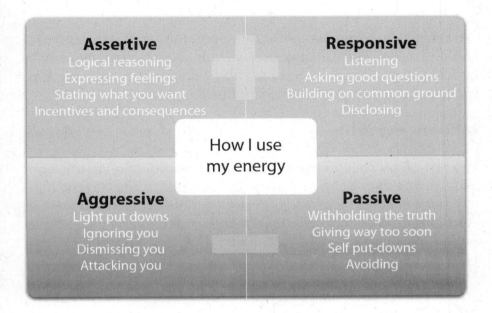

My Agenda | Your Agenda

Assertive
Logical reasoning
Expressing feelings
Stating what you want
Incentives and consequences

Responsive
Listening
Asking good questions
Building on common ground
Disclosing

How I use
my energy

Aggressive
Light put downs
Ignoring you
Dismissing you
Attacking you

Passive
Withholding the truth
Giving way too soon
Self put-downs
Avoiding

Figure 2 Model courtesy of Sheppard Moscow (www.sheppardmoscow.com)

A word about negative influence

To strengthen our ability to lead and influence others requires that we become fluent in the eight positive behaviors in the top half of the model (figure 2). It is, of course, possible to influence and get things done by using negative behaviors, such as those illustrated in the bottom quadrants. It is all too common, particularly at very senior levels of management, to see both men and women misusing their positional power by using aggression as a means of getting what they want. Putting down other people, ignoring or dismissing their contributions, and verbally attacking others is about managing through fear and is, in my view, bullying, not leadership.

Negative influence can also take a passive form. Withholding the truth when it could make a positive difference, giving way too soon and not standing our ground for what we believe in, chronically putting ourselves down, and avoiding uncomfortable situations that need to be addressed, are all behaviors that reduce our ability to influence and diminish our credibility as leaders.

We are all human and we will at times find ourselves behaving passively or aggressively. If, however, we are serious about becoming good leaders and operating successfully within today's organizations, we need to develop our ability to influence positively.

Influencing skills

The rest of this chapter will provide a brief introduction to the eight positive influence behaviors that will, if you become proficient in using them, enable you to lead others even more effectively and meet some of the challenges of the *unwritten rules*. By the experiential nature of behavioral change, the best way to strengthen existing behaviors and develop new behaviors is not through reading a book. The intention here, therefore, is first to provide intellectual insight and understanding, such that you will broaden your awareness and thinking about how you currently influence and how you might further develop your skills. Second, I hope to motivate you to take these skills seriously as part of your ongoing professional development. To that end, I will include some suggested resources at the end of the chapter.

The "Pull" Behaviors

Listening

Asking good questions

Building on common ground

Disclosing

The orientation for these four behaviors is to involve and collaborate with others so that together you gain commitment and achieve your desired end results. It is appropriate to use these behaviors when:

- You are open to influence about what or how something can be done.

- You want to gain commitment rather than just compliance to a course of action.

- You want to build trust so that you can work together more effectively.

- You want to motivate and excite people around a vision.

- You want to understand and work with resistance.

- You want to break a deadlocked situation or diffuse aggressive behavior.

Behavior #1: Listening

I would like to introduce you to Vicki and Elizabeth:

Vicki has an open-door policy. She values the importance of being available to support her team and her colleagues when they need her.

Although she is frequently overworked and rushing from one task and one meeting to the next, she always has time for people. Imagine Vicki's surprise when her 360-degree feedback reveals that her team and colleagues don't feel that she listens to them. Her intention is certainly to be available and to hear them, but somehow she is having a different impact. She doesn't understand the feedback she is getting.

Elizabeth is delighted to be part of a senior executive group that is setting strategy for an important and high-profile project. The group is composed of predominantly male colleagues, some of their bosses, and her own boss. Elizabeth knows the traps of operating in this kind of group and has thought carefully about what she wants to contribute and how she wants to make an impact. She knows that she will need to use strong, assertive behaviors to get heard and be taken seriously. After six weeks on the project, her manager takes her aside and tells her that if she isn't prepared to work more cooperatively with the other team members, he will need to take her off the project. Elizabeth is confused, wasn't she behaving just like everyone else on the team?

If you were able to observe Vicki and Elizabeth in these two work situations here is what you would see:

Vicki

Vicki is working at her computer. One of her direct reports enters the office and asks for five minutes. Vicki invites him to sit down and continues to tap away on her computer.

Her direct report explains the issue.

Vicki stops tapping on the computer, but frequently looks toward the monitor screen, particularly responding to the sound of an arriving e-mail.

Her direct report continues to explain the issue.

The phone rings, Vicki holds up her hand for her direct report to pause a moment, and she answers the phone. Vicki rushes through the phone conversation and then tells her direct report to continue.

Her direct report continues.

Vicki's assistant puts her head around the door to tell her that her 11:00 a.m. meeting is here. Vicki interrupts her direct report to give him the quick bit of advice that she thinks he needs to resolve his issue and tells him to catch her later if he needs to talk some more.

Her direct report leaves her office and when out of earshot mutters, "That was a waste of time."

Vicki continues with her next meeting, during which she checks her smart phone three times and finds herself missing parts of the meeting because she is distracted by a worrying e-mail that has just popped onto her screen.

After a day of similar interactions Vicki is tired, but satisfied with the number of tasks she has managed to get off her list. She has made time for everyone who needed it and she would be shocked if she knew that many of the people she interacted with had left feeling that they had not really been heard. Vicki's colleagues report that she has many strengths … listening is not one of them.

Elizabeth

Elizabeth sits at the conference table halfway through the weekly project meeting. She is the only woman in the room. As usual, she has strong views about the topic on the table and she stands her ground, clearly expressing her views and opinions, strongly stating her expectations about what needs to happen, without being afraid to voice her frustration and disappointment when some of her colleagues do not agree with her. Elizabeth has been to an assertiveness course for women that has helped her develop these behaviors, so she is now confident in expressing herself in meetings with strong, somewhat domineering men. Her ability to stand her ground in such company is one of the reasons she has been identified as a high-potential candidate for an even bigger job. Unfortunately, although Elizabeth demonstrates excellent assertive behaviors, it is the *only* type of behavior she uses. Her consistent pushing for her own agenda (because she knows she is right and just needs to convince the others to understand) results either in her colleagues resentfully backing down (which she thinks is a good result) or in an escalating battle. Elizabeth's colleagues think she is aggressive and have complained about her to her boss.

Vicki and Elizabeth's colleagues do not feel heard. Vicki is labeled a "poor listener," even though she thinks this is one of her strengths. Elizabeth is considered "aggressive" because, even though she uses her assertive behaviors well, she is overusing them and not demonstrating that she has heard her colleagues or values their contributions. Improving their ability to demonstrate to others that they are listening would make life easier for Vicki, Elizabeth, and their colleagues. It would also enable them to get things done with others, while maintaining or building better working relationships.

Demonstrating you have heard versus passive listening

It's not enough to passively listen to others if we want to be influential and have a positive impact. Vicki might well have the capability to listen while multi-tasking, just as Elizabeth might be listening in between pushing for what she wants. The trouble is neither of them is demonstrating this in any way that their colleagues could have a clue that they are listening. The test of influential listening is whether others leave the conversation feeling heard and understood. We don't necessarily need to agree with each other, but we all need our views and opinions to be heard and at least considered if we are to work well together.

Listening is not a passive activity. There's a lot going on when we not only listen well, but also demonstrate that we have heard what others have to say. Some easy steps to listening in a way that demonstrates to others that you are doing so is to give full attention, summarize what you are hearing, make explicit your assumptions or interpretations, and reflect the feelings you are picking up from the other person.

Giving full attention

Stop what you are doing and give your full attention to the person you are listening to. If you can't do this, I recommend that you arrange to speak with the person at a time when you can do it rather than half-listening while doing other tasks. Giving your full attention means clearing your mind and focusing fully on the other person and what he or she is saying. Listen with your ears and your body to everything that is said. This means turning to face the person, engaging in good eye contact, nodding, smiling if appropriate, and generally looking like you are paying attention. If you become distracted, simply bring your focus and attention back to the other person. Think of someone you consider to be a great listener. I'll wager that when that person is listening to you, you feel that you have his or her complete attention.

Giving full attention when we are listening to others is more of an orientation than a skill. We all have the capability to stop what we are doing and focus on what others have to say. It simply requires an awareness of what we are doing and the impact it has, and a decision to really listen to someone or not. If we have the orientation that we respect our colleagues and what they have to say (even if we don't necessarily agree with them) then it is easier to move onto their agendas and give them our full attention.

Summarizing

Summarizing is a form of mental note taking. When you have listened to the speaker making a few different points, summarize what you think you have heard. This does not mean parroting back everything the other person has said (which is very irritating). It means taking the detail of their conversation and presenting it back as a concise summary. This not only enables you to check the accuracy of your understanding, it also demonstrates to the other person that you have really heard him or her. If you are working with someone who talks a lot, you might need to politely interrupt in order to be able to summarize what you have heard so far. To do this, try using words such as:

"Can I just check my understanding of what you're saying ... "

Or

"Let me summarize what I am hearing ... "

Interrupting and summarizing in this way also enables you to help the person get back to the point if he or she has started to digress.

Interpreting

Sometimes, when you have listened well, you may be able to make interpretations of what the other person has said or identify implications from his or her statements. Interpretation or implication statements play back to the other person something that he or she hasn't actually said, but that is implied in what the person is saying. It can be very effective to check out interpretations that you are making to assess their accuracy, highlight something to the other person that he or she may not be aware of, and to demonstrate again that you are listening and understanding.

Example:

You have been paying full attention and summarizing what your colleague has been describing. You think what he is saying adds up to a particular conclusion that he hasn't yet stated, in this case, that he won't be able to deliver the project by the due date. You put your interpretation on the table:

"From what you have said, it sounds like you don't think you will be able to deliver the project on time."

Or

"The implication of what you are saying is that you won't hit the due date."

If your interpretation is correct your colleague will feel that you are really listening to and understanding his situation. You are also likely to move the conversation to new depths through identifying implications of which the other person may not be fully aware. If you find you have misinterpreted what the speaker has said or he backs out of the implication because he doesn't like it, it still enables you to check out an interpretation that you have already made and assess its accuracy.

Checking assumptions

Assumptions are beliefs or ideas that we hold to be true, usually based on our own view of the world. For example, if you are listening to someone talking about a problem, you might assume that he or she wants you to solve it because, in your view, why else would the person be talking to you. We are often advised not to make assumptions, which, of course, is impossible. What you can do, however, is check out the assumptions you are making as part of listening and understanding the person you are working with.

Example:

"I'm assuming that you would like me to give you some advice, is that correct?"

Or

"Can I check my understanding? Would it be most helpful for me to listen and explore how you're thinking about this? Or would you like me to offer some advice?"

Being aware of and checking the assumptions you are making will not only enable you to deepen your understanding of others' ideas, views, opinions, etc., it will also help the person you are listening to think more clearly and feel listened to and heard.

Reflecting feelings

There are conflicting views about expressing feelings in the workplace. It can be a particularly difficult area for women given the stereotype that women can be "too emotional" (and, by implication, not good leadership material). As a component of good listening, however, what you are doing is enabling *others* to express their feelings in a way that might be helpful to them. As with all of the pull behaviors, this is not about you, it's about them.

When you are listening to someone, you may become aware of some emotion that the speaker is experiencing, for example, embarrassment, anger, joy, etc. It can sometimes be helpful to reflect back what you are seeing to enable the other person to more easily express the emotion.

For example:

"You sound angry about how she treated you in that meeting."

Or

"It sounds like you're excited, but a bit nervous about the new job."

Expressing feelings is a behavior that many people find difficult, especially in the workplace, but the emotions are always there, expressed or not. When you are listening effectively to others it can be very helpful to recognize and help others to express their emotions to enable them to gain insights and release energy.

Orientation

Good listening is not a collection of techniques. To be a good listener you must be able to change your focus from yourself to another person. Your orientation is about understanding the person in front of you. It is not about trying to solve the person's problems or asking questions that push him or her in a particular direction that you want to go. It's about respecting that the other person may have different views and opinions from your own and still being willing to listen and trying to understand the person's position. It does not mean that you have to agree with him or her, but simply to demonstrate that you understand how he or she thinks and feels.

Why use it as part of your influence repertoire?

You will usually have more success in influencing people, particularly in difficult situations, if you have built a good relationship with them. Becoming a good listener is one of the most effective ways to build relationships with other people. Taking the time to listen and genuinely trying to understand is a rare skill in today's hectic business environment. If you can learn to listen well and actively demonstrate that you are doing so, it will form the basis of all of your other influence behaviors.

In addition, influence is a reciprocal process. If you want other people to listen to you and take your thoughts and feelings seriously, you must be prepared to do the same for them. And finally, listening to and understanding another person will give you information about how this person thinks and operates, which becomes crucial when you need to influence them in some way.

Going back to Vicki and Elizabeth.... What would help Vicki is to decide if she has the time to genuinely listen to the person in front of her and if she doesn't, arrange a later time to meet with them. Half-listening while she is doing other things does more harm than good in terms of her impact as a colleague and as a leader. What would help Elizabeth is to continue using her strong assertive skills, but to add in skilful listening, so that she is more balanced in her behavior. Both Vicki and Elizabeth would benefit from developing their abilities to demonstrate that they have genuinely heard what others are saying to them by using all of the components of listening if they want to influence their colleagues in a way that maintains or builds relationships.

Summary

As a leader, you need to be able to involve and collaborate with others by responding appropriately to their ideas, views, opinions, concerns, feelings, etc. Listening and demonstrating that you have heard is an essential component of this. It involves:

- Giving your full attention

- Summarizing what you are hearing

- Voicing any interpretations you are making

- Checking your assumptions

- Reflecting back feelings that you think might be helpful for the other person to express

I recommend that you try practicing these different components, first in less demanding situations, then working up to situations where you feel under more pressure.

Behavior #2: Asking good questions

A natural companion behavior to listening is asking good questions, which is easy if you have been listening well. The intention behind asking good questions is to deepen your understanding of others' ideas, views, opinions, expectations, etc. Asking good questions and demonstrating that you have heard shows that you are interested in what others think and what they have to say. Exploring where others are coming from and what they have to contribute brings people together through shared understanding, helps to avoid or overcome misunderstandings, brings new ideas to the surface, supports problem solving and can help to resolve conflict. As a leader, if you listen well and ask good, exploring questions you will not only fully utilize the talent around you, you will also draw people toward wanting to work with you.

You can develop your skill in this area by experimenting with asking four different types of questions that explore how others are thinking and which deepen your understanding of your colleagues situation, issues, ideas, opinions, etc.

Types of questions

There are four types of questions you can use to deepen your understanding when you work with others:

1. Information questions

2. Clarification questions

3. Implication questions

4. Discrepancy questions

Information questions

Information questions are used to expand and deepen your understanding of what the other person is telling you. They are usually open questions that start with the words "what," "where," "when," "how," or "why." For example:

Statement:	"I can't meet the deadline for this work."
Information question:	"Why not?"
Reply:	"There isn't enough time to complete all of the regulatory procedures."
Information question:	"What procedures require more time?"
Reply:	"All of the tests being done by our U.K. subsidiary."
Information question:	"Why are their tests taking longer?"
Reply:	"We have a problem with the equipment in the U.K. plant."
Information question:	"When did you first become aware of this?"

As you can see, each information question expands your understanding of the situation. If, however, we continue using only information questions the other person is likely to feel interrogated and will probably start getting defensive. Occasionally summarizing what the other person has told you, checking assumptions you are making, and reflecting feelings (demonstrating you have heard) will help to make this a joint exploration of the situation, rather than an interrogation.

Clarification questions

These are questions you can use to clarify information you have received that you don't fully understand.

Example:

Statement:	"You didn't get the job, because we thought that you needed more leadership presence."
Clarification question:	"What do you mean by 'leadership presence'?"

Example:

Statement:	"We need to develop a more robust PDP"
Clarification question:	"What's a PDP?"

Asking clarification questions ensures that you and everyone else involved in the meeting are on the same page and clearly understand what is being discussed.

Implication questions

If you notice an unspoken implication in something you are being told, you can ask an implication question to verify whether or not the implication exists.

Example:

Statement: "On this occasion he treated me with respect."

Unspoken implication: On other occasions he treated her with disrespect.

Implication question: "Is this unusual?"

Example:

Statement: "People really took notice of what you had to say in this meeting."

Unspoken implication: For some reason, people haven't taken notice in other meetings.

Implication question: "Did I do something different in this meeting that made others take more notice?"

To notice and check out implications in what others are saying deepens your understanding of both the situation and the other person.

Discrepancy questions

If you are given conflicting information you can ask a discrepancy question to determine if some or all of the information is incorrect, or if there is missing information that would clarify the discrepancy.

Example:

Statement: "We think you have the capacity to progress rapidly in this company, but you won't be part of the high-potential group this year."

Discrepancy:	You have the capacity to progress rapidly, but will not be put into an identified group for promotion.
Discrepancy question:	"Given that you think I have the capacity to progress rapidly, why am I not going to be part of the high-potential group?"

Example:

Statement:	"Susan is the right person to lead this team, although her people skills aren't very good."
Discrepancy:	Susan has poor people skills and she is the right person to lead a team.
Discrepancy question:	"If Susan has poor people skills, why do you think she is the right person to lead the team?"

It's easy and quite common to ignore discrepancies in what others say or make assumptions about what we think they intended. It is more effective and safer to explore a discrepancy, rather than assume we know what the other person meant.

The real skill in asking questions that explore what others bring to the table is to do it in a way that stays focused on their agenda, rather than moving to your own. This is not to say that you lose your own agenda, but that you are able to put it to one side and invest sufficient time to understand the people you are working with. Your intention in doing this is to embark on a joint exploration with others to understand their thinking, their issues, their ideas and perhaps their feelings. Leading teams of people works best if we utilize all of the resources of the team. As a leader, listening and asking good questions enables us to do this.

In our previous examples, if Vicki's colleagues see that she is able to park her own agenda for awhile and give her full attention to them by listening and asking good questions, they will be more likely to achieve better outcomes together. If Elizabeth is able to promote her own agenda while demonstrating the ability to listen and explore others' agendas, she is more likely to positively influence the project team to achieve good results together.

Behavior #3: Finding common ground and building a shared vision

Rachel is an excellent critical thinker. She is valued in her organization for her quick mind, her logic and her ability to incisively identify key issues—and, particularly, key problems. She has aspirations to move from her position as vice president to become general manager of her division of a large multinational company. She is stuck in her current position, however, because she is seen as a "doer"—a person who gets things done, rather than a particularly strong leader of people.

Rachel's boss, Susan, is also an excellent critical thinker. But unlike Rachel, she has also developed the ability to bring people together around a common vision. Rachel knows that Susan is able to work with the people she leads in a way that she cannot, but she can't put her finger on exactly what it is that Susan does that is so effective in getting everyone's commitment to common goals.

One of the reasons that Susan is a good leader is that she purposely brings her people together by creating a shared vision that is built on their common interests, ideas, aspirations, goals and values. If you could break down into discrete components what Susan is doing, here is what you would see:

Identifying the common ground

Susan is intentional about discovering the areas that she and her people have in common, so that they then have something positive to build on. Her purpose in doing this is to enable people to work together in collaborative endeavour toward desired end results. Her ability to listen and ask exploring questions enables her to identify where they have common interests and agreement. She uses positive language and energy, so that the people around her often feel that anything is possible when they work with her. If you could watch Susan when she establishes common ground with her colleagues, you would see her being lively and animated; her voice is positive and enthusiastic; and she uses words such as:

"So we are all agreed that …"

"It seems we both believe in … "

"I agree with you … "

"Let's look at what we agree on …"

"That's something we have in common … "

"Let's remind ourselves of what we are all trying to achieve here…"

If you were to observe meetings when Susan is not around, you would see her colleagues often focusing on the differences and disagreements that divide them. Certainly differences must be identified and resolved before many projects can be successfully completed. Susan has learned, however, that there is more than one approach in doing this and finds that they often gain more success if she and her colleagues first identify and build on the common ground that they share.

Levels of common ground

If you want to practice this behavior, you can try establishing common ground on different levels: everyday life and interests; views and opinions; goals and values. At which level you establish common ground with others depends on the time available, the situation, and your current depth of relationship.

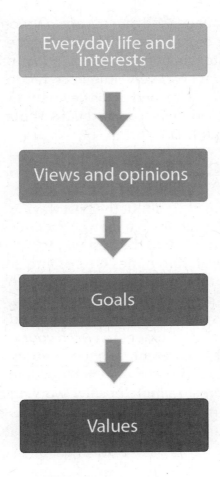

Level 1: Everyday life and interests

This is usually the easiest and most superficial level on which to find common ground with others. For example, discovering that you share a mutual acquaintance, a shared interest in sports or culture, a child of a similar age, an interest in current events, and so on. Finding common ground with your colleagues around everyday life and interests establishes the early stages of relationship building. Women who are not sports fans sometimes experience difficulties in finding common interests with their male colleagues. In my experience, however, it is nearly always possible to find some areas of common interest, if you are prepared to listen and ask exploring questions. Many years ago, as a senior manager and one of very few women at my level in a financial services organization, I was often seated beside the head of sales at corporate functions. He was a serious man, prone to long silences, with whom I had very little in common. After patient exploring and listening, I learned of his devotion to his daughter and, subsequently, we had many conversations about our children and built an easy, pleasant relationship.

Level 2: Views and opinions

We all have our own ideas about the best ways to achieve tasks and goals. The usual format for meetings is to discuss differing views and opinions in order to find the best way forward. Sometimes this approach works well; sometimes it turns into a battle of who can push the hardest to win the day; and sometimes groups simply get stuck on their differing views and opinions. An alternative approach often helps to bring people together and break a deadlock. Consciously listen for the extent to which your views and opinions are similar rather than different. Calling attention to where you have some commonality and agreement and building on them through summarizing can create a more positive working climate. If you are the person in the meeting who can do this, you are likely to draw people toward you and stand out as a skilled influencer.

Level 3: Goals

An important aspect of being a leader is the ability to establish shared goals around which people can align. Sometimes people in the same organization forget that they are working toward common goals. Drawing attention to this can refocus the conversation in a positive way. It is usually possible to listen for and identify shared goals, even where there are differences in the ways and means of achieving them.

As a general manager, Susan's direct reports represent different departments. Sometimes they get into battles that are clearly more about protecting their own territory than creating a way to move forward as a whole organization. Part of Susan's skill as a good leader is her ability to see this and help them take a step back to look at the bigger picture and the common goals that they all have.

Level 4: Values

Knowing what we stand for and aligning our behavior with our values are core components of good leadership. Values are also the deepest and most fundamental level at which we can establish common ground with others. If we are able to find values that we share with our colleagues, we can more likely face differences and conflict without permanent damage to the relationship. For example, if Susan has established with a colleague that they both value honesty and they have gradually built their working relationship on this fundamental connection, they are more likely to be able to reconnect after serious differences of opinion, because they value the candid behavior that they both bring to the table.

I Imagine at this stage you may think, "This is all well and good, but building good working relationships based on common ground takes time"—something that you may be short of. It's true that finding and building on common ground at a values level requires more investment than connecting with your colleagues at the level of everyday interests. Many leaders I have coached agree that establishing common ground and building strong working relationships with colleagues is helpful, but often claim that they simply don't have the time to invest.

Leading requires the ability to create a vision that people can organize around and move toward. If people feel little connection either to their leader or her vision, they are unlikely to commit the time and energy to achieve it. Good leaders invest the time to find common ground and build a shared vision with their people. It is possible to do this in everyday situations by consciously looking for and explicitly stating the common ground that you see, as opposed to getting stuck on the differences of opinion. This is not an additional, time-consuming activity, but rather a different way of operating in everyday interactions.

Building a shared vision

Did you know that CEOs believe that the ability to communicate a strong vision is the most critical factor for success? The Center for Creative Leadership gathered data from 146 CEOs between September 2007 and September 2008. They were asked to select the top five factors for success from a list of thirteen items. Seventy-five percent of the CEOs ranked the ability to communicate a strong vision as the single most critical factor.

It is very difficult to build a shared vision with others until we have established common ground. Many leaders make the mistake of creating their own vision and then trying to "sell" it to those they are leading in the hope that they will enlist enthusiastic followers. It is far more effective to create a shared vision with others by building on the goals and values that you have in common. The behaviors of finding common ground and building a shared vision, therefore, go hand-in-hand.

I have found that some people avoid these behaviors because they think that their vision has to be grand and delivered with the skill of a great speaker. Certainly people like Martin Luther King, Jr., and Barack Obama have moved millions of people with their eloquent ability to unite people around a shared vision. But in an everyday sense, we can all build on the common ground that unites us as people working toward common goals in organizations. Creating a shared vision can be achieved between individuals, members of a small group or a whole organization. It can be a small or a grand vision, as long as it is shared. And although it needs to be built with enthusiasm and energy, this can be done in a fairly low-key way right through to a major speech. This is a behavior that anyone can use who is interested in joining with others to create a desired end result.

If you want to practice creating a shared vision, try building on the common ground you have generated to create a positive picture of a way forward that appeals to the interests, goals, and values of the people you are working with. Ensure that you demonstrate energy and enthusiasm for what you believe in and use positive language such as:

"Just imagine what it would be like if we could be the first to market with this product."

"I can see us this time next year, when we have exceeded all of the goals we have set."

"What I see us creating together is a dynamic, expert team that becomes a role model for other project teams in the company."

"The results will be incredible, if we can pull this off."

The success of this approach relies upon appealing to what you have discovered you all have in common, rather than creating a vision that appeals to you as a leader and hoping you can sell it to others.

Behavior #4: Disclosing

"Disclosing" is the final behavior on the responsive side of the model. The intention behind this behavior is to be collaborative and to build trust. Very simply, the behavior involves being open by disclosing relevant facts, thoughts and feelings that you believe will be helpful to others.

Examples:

"Something that you need to know about this particular client is that he doesn't like doing business with women because ..."

"I have found myself in a similar difficult situation and I dealt with it by ..."

"Here's some information that has not yet been announced, but it will help you by ..."

"My thinking behind wanting to do this is ..."

"I'm feeling unsure about how to move forward with this ... "

Women leaders who favor strong, assertive behaviors often see disclosure as, at best, unnecessary and, at worst, weak—particularly if it involves disclosing feelings of distress or uncertainty. As a woman working within the structure of the *unwritten rules*, you need to be mindful about what you disclose and to whom. Trust needs to be built gradually and knowing whom you can trust and at what level you can disclose requires awareness of the culture and how things work in your organization. With this health warning in mind, it is helpful to know that disclosing is a key behavior in building trust and encouraging openness in return. It will also help your colleagues to see you as more "human" if your tendency is to present a very invulnerable and polished exterior to the world.

In building a good working relationship someone needs to make the first move in disclosing information or feelings. This can make us feel vulnerable and can even feel risky in certain situations, because we do not know how other people might respond. However, an appropriate disclosure often results in the other person respecting you for giving information that you did not have to disclose and then being more willing to reciprocate. In this way, a more effective working relationship is formed.

Using this behavior

As a general rule, disclosing is best developed as a stepped process. Sudden unilateral lunges into profound disclosure should be avoided. They can generate distrust, apprehension, amusement, and/or embarrassment. (You may have had the experience, as I have, of being trapped on an airplane next to someone who wants to tell you his or her life story before you have even taken off). What and how much to disclose depends on the situation and the level of existing trust.

Linda is a successful, highly competent leader in an organization where she is heavily outnumbered by men. She is seen as a tough professional who gets results. Some people like her and some fear her. She pays little or no attention to the sometimes sexist behavior of her colleagues that she knows is generated from gender stereotyping. If you observed Linda's behavior on a daily basis, you would see her listening well, but using predominantly strong, assertive behaviors. She supports her decisions and recommendations with logical reasons and she is clear about her expectations of others. Linda is a possible candidate for an even more senior position and she is working with an executive coach to prepare for the transition.

Linda's development with her executive coach is based mainly on the responsive (pull) side of the behavioral model. She is building on her good ability to listen by learning to explore others' agendas, as opposed to asking questions related to her own agenda, which reportedly make her colleagues feel interrogated. She is discovering the effectiveness of finding common ground and building a shared vision. She has always done this with her direct reports but she had never transferred this skill to working with her colleagues on the senior management team. And she is experimenting with disclosing more of her thoughts and feelings to others, something she initially felt very apprehensive about. Linda is discovering that the respect others have for her competence and assertiveness allows her to sometimes disclose mistakes or uncertainty, while retaining her credibility. In fact, her colleagues report that she is becoming easier to work with and to follow as a leader, because they see her as "more human." This also allows them to trust her enough to disclose some of their mistakes and uncertainty to her.

If disclosing is a new or fairly unused behavior for you, start by practicing giving helpful information, then move onto thoughts and feelings as the relationship builds and you glean evidence that the other person appreciates your disclosures and can be trusted. The thing to remember with this behavior is that you are disclosing facts, thoughts, and feelings that are **related to the other person's agenda.** This means that the disclosure is intended to help and support the other person in some way.

The "Push" Behaviors

Logical reasoning

Expressing feelings

Stating what you want

Incentives and consequences

Leading requires not only that we involve and collaborate with others, but also that we are able to state clearly what we want, need, and expect from those we are working with. As leaders we need to be clear about what needs to happen in order to get our desired end results and be able to express ourselves in an assertive, rather than an aggressive, way. Using assertive behaviors is often more challenging for women because stating clearly what we want goes against the stereotypical expectations that women should be caring and responsive. It is even more important, therefore, that women leaders develop expertise in using the push behaviors in a way that impacts assertively rather than aggressively and that they become fluent in combining them with the responsive pull behaviors.

It is appropriate to use the push behaviors of logical reasoning, expressing feelings, stating what you want, and incentives and consequences when:

- You are clear about what you want or what you think needs to happen.

- You have strong views and want to influence a decision or others' behaviors.

- The people you are influencing need or want clear guidance and direction.

- You have logic, evidence, or data to support your views.

- You need to assert your own rights as a leader and as a woman.

Behavior #5: Logical reasoning

This behavior consists of expressing your views and opinions, supported by logical reasoning, with the intention of moving things forward. It is the behavior most used in organizations, but it is not often used well. For example, think of the number of meetings you have sat through where the agenda is overrun because there are lengthy exchanges of views and opinions with very little progress. Recall the situations where your mind has wandered to other things because the person talking was taking too long to get to the point. And remember the last time you failed to get a satisfactory result from a meeting because you weren't clear about exactly what it was that you wanted as an outcome. Improving your skill in logical reasoning will not only enable you to influence more effectively in situations such as these, it will also enable you to stand out from the majority of people who use this behavior with less skill.

As with all of the push behaviors, the key is clarity and conciseness. There are two simple components to logical reasoning:

1. A clear, concise statement of your view, opinion, idea, suggestion, or proposal.

2. A maximum of three supporting reasons.

It looks something like these examples:

"I have an idea. Let's make the training mandatory rather than optional. In that way we can ensure consistent quality across all parts of the organization."

"I have a suggestion. My suggestion is that we move production to the Montreal plant because we have more capacity there, it is closer to our biggest client and it will reduce transport costs."

"I would like to make a proposal. I propose we convene an additional board meeting before the holidays, and I have three reasons for suggesting this. First, we need to get a statement out to the media quickly before rumors start to affect the share price. Second, we need to jointly discuss and address the concerns raised in this letter from our main shareholder. And last, it is likely that the regulator will be onto this quickly and we need to prepare our response. What do you think?"

If we analyze the above statements, you will notice that each example starts with a suggestion or proposal. Starting with a proposal before giving your reasons is helpful in three ways. First, you need to have thought through what you are suggesting in order to make the proposal—it helps you to think clearly about what you want. Second, if you start reasoning before giving a clear proposal, people may become confused about the point you are trying to make and stop listening. And last, if you put your reasons up front, others might start arguing with your reasons before understanding your main proposal.

You will also notice in the above examples that there is a short statement before each proposal that labels the behavior you are about to use: "I have a suggestion," "I have an idea," "I would like to make a proposal." This is a very effective method of signaling to others that you have something to say and is a good way to get their attention before presenting your case. It is a particularly useful technique for breaking into noisy discussions and ensuring that people are listening before you present your ideas.

As illustrated by the above examples, when using this behavior I recommend that you limit your reasons to a maximum of three, even if you have many more good reasons to support your case. Select your two or three strongest reasons and keep any others that you have in reserve, in case you need additional logic or supporting data as part of a discussion. This is important for two reasons: first, using too many reasons and giving too much detail becomes boring and turns people off; second, if you use every reason you can think of, your weakest reasons are likely to be attacked and used to undermine your case. If you are unsure whether your three good reasons will be sufficient and are tempted to give more, a simple technique is to deliver your proposal, with three concise reasons and then ask your listeners if those are sufficient or would they like to hear more? I guarantee that, in most cases, your listeners will have had enough, if you have given just a few good reasons—particularly if you are talking to senior management.

Positive orientation

People who excel at logical reasoning often have a natural ability to critically evaluate. It is counterproductive, however, to be constantly criticizing others' views and opinions. If you do this you are likely to be experienced as a negative, rather than a positive influence. No one enjoys or is motivated by constant negative evaluations. If you find yourself frequently using phrases such as:

"That won't work because…"

"We've tried that before and it didn't work…"

"We can't do that because…"

"Ah, but …"

you are likely to be creating a negative climate around you. People will be less motivated to both share their ideas with you and follow you as a leader. This is not to say that you must never use critical evaluation, just that you use it sparingly and thoughtfully. You might also like to try out the following phrases as more positive options:

"Yes, and we could also try…"

"Another way to look at this is…"

"Alternatively, we could have a look at…"

Good leaders create a positive, can-do climate around them. One of the many ways to do this is to always be moving things forward with positive views and opinions, rather than frequently criticizing or complaining.

Responding to others' logical reasoning

When others are using push energy and presenting their views and opinions, we are often hooked into responding with our own push energy by countering with our own logical reasoning. This often accelerates the discussion into an argument or battle. If you want to be influential and move things forward, often the most effective response to someone else's views is to:

- Listen and demonstrate that you have understood and that you respect the person's views.

- Ask good questions to deepen your understanding of his or her position.

- Explicitly look for and state any common ground that you can build on if the person's view aligns with yours in some way.

Even if you do not agree with what someone else is saying, it is usually more positively influential to demonstrate you have heard and understood the person and deepen your understanding of his or her position before presenting an alternative view.

Situational flexibility

Expressing your views strongly enough to be taken seriously requires differing amounts of strength, depending on the situation and the people you are working with. This means that you need to assess the situation and continually adjust the strength of your message. The illustration below gives examples that you can try out:

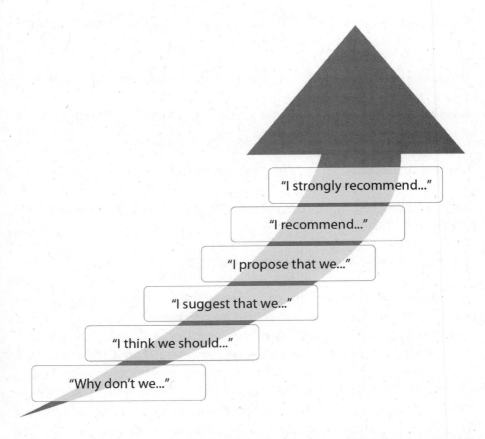

For example, if you are working with a trusted colleague and longtime friend, you are more likely to use phrases at the "lighter" end of the scale, such as "Why don't we … " or "I think we should …" because this is appropriate for the relationship and sufficient to influence the situation. On the other hand, if you are attempting to influence a pushy group of senior leaders, you are likely to need to work at the stronger end of the scale using phrases such as " I recommend …" or " I strongly recommend …".

If you want to improve your logical reasoning, I suggest that you try using the following structure because it will enable you to be clear, concise and to the point.

Label your behavior:	"I have a suggestion/proposal/recommendation."
Propose precisely:	"I suggest/propose/recommend that we ... "
Reason concisely:	"I have two reasons: my first reason is ... my second reason is ... "
Invite a response:	"What do you think?"

As a colleague of mine used to say, "Propose precisely, reason concisely, and shut up nicely."

Behavior #6: Expressing feelings

Positively influencing a situation or another person through skillful expression of feelings is a rare skill in organizations. It's also a potential minefield for women because of the "emotional woman" stereotype. Remember President Richard Nixon's comment from Chapter One: "I don't think a woman should be in any government job whatsoever ... The reason why I do is mainly because they are erratic ... and emotional. Men are erratic and emotional, too, but the point is a woman is more likely to be."[73] Unfortunately, this stereotype is still deeply embedded in our culture, which makes many women quite sensibly wary about expressing emotions in the workplace.

In terms of positive influence, there is either confusion or unawareness about the difference between expressing feelings to positively influence a person or a situation and emotional outbursts that nearly always have a negative impact. Developing the skill to express emotion to either change a situation that you don't like or reinforce a situation that you do like can be a powerful tool in your repertoire of influencing skills—if you know how to use it.

Expressing feelings as a positive influence style is NOT about getting emotional. In fact, the skill is to express the emotion you are genuinely feeling without actually getting into the emotion itself. It is about paying attention to how you are feeling in a given situation, making a decision about how you want to influence the situation and expressing your feelings in a way that is honest, controlled and effective. Expressing feelings as an influence style can be used to reinforce a positive situation that you would like to build on or to address a negative situation that needs to change. Here's what it looks like if it is done well. You might say:

Expressed feeling:	"I'm absolutely **delighted** with the new format you've created for the monthly report."
Intention:	To recognize good work and encourage its continuation.
Expressed feelings:	I'm both **pleased** and **impressed** by the way you have stepped up to the plate and taken on additional responsibility for this project."
Intention:	To recognize good performance and encourage its continuation.
Expressed feelings:	"When you continually interrupt me in this meeting and never let me finish I feel **ignored** and **disrespected**."
Intention:	To call attention to destructive behavior and get the other person to stop it.
Expressed feeling:	"When you take my ideas and present them as your own I feel **angry**."
Intention:	To identify behavior you don't like and want the other person to stop.

Expressing feelings in this way, to change a situation that you don't like or to reinforce a situation that you do like tends to have a strong impact, stronger than using logical reasoning for example. This is because you are engaging the other person on an emotional level as opposed to a cerebral level. The person you are influencing is likely to feel a stronger push when you express your feelings, rather than when you push through logically reasoning.

When you express your feelings with the intention of reinforcing good work as in the first two examples above, it often has a powerful and positive impact. People in organizations often comment that they receive more negative evaluation than positive from their boss. (Children often have the same complaint about their parents). Expressing genuine positive emotion that is both accurate and honest goes a long way toward motivating others to want to continue performing well.

Most of us naturally find it easier to express feelings when we are positively reinforcing something we like. It takes more courage to use this behavior to influence situations that we don't like and want to change. This is because we are unsure or afraid of the response we are likely to get from the person we are trying to influence. My experience of expressing my feelings in situations such as these is that the other person usually apologizes, often quite shocked and alarmed that their behavior has had such a negative impact. For example, when I expressed my anger and disappointment to a colleague who failed to stand by me in a difficult situation, he apologized and the ensuing conversation triggered a helpful discussion about how we could work together more effectively. If, however, you are working in an organizational culture where people do not care about each other to the extent that a colleague's feelings are irrelevant, this influence style clearly won't be effective. The only advice I can give in this situation is to find somewhere else to work where people have some care and regard for each other.

Meet Kelley and Sylvanna:

Kelley tries to keep her emotions under tight control in the workplace, particularly with her peers and her boss. It's not that she cuts herself off from emotion, but rather that she doesn't see a place for expressing it without being labeled "an emotional woman" and she is afraid that if she does express how she sometimes feels at work the dam might break, releasing an emotional outburst. Kelley hates the fact that her suppressed feelings result in the occasional meltdown, either with her team or at home with her husband and children. She also suspects that it is adversely affecting her health, but doesn't know how to change this pattern of behavior.

Sylvanna has no problem expressing her emotions at work, so much so that her team walk on eggshells around her, never knowing what mood they might encounter at any moment of the day. She frequently reduces team members to tears with her cutting comments and emotional outbursts. At the same time, she is just as likely to bubble over with positive emotion when she is pleased and something has gone well. Her team never feels sure about where they stand with her or what to expect. Most of them are looking for another job.

Kelley's fear of emotional outbursts is, paradoxically, causing her emotional outbursts with her team and with her family. Her unexpressed emotions with her colleagues and her boss will either cause her stress and illness if they stay suppressed or they will burst out in situations where she feels safer (with her team and family.) She would be healthier and more effective if she learned to express her feelings, *without getting emotional,* with the people who are triggering them.

Sylvanna currently behaves with little regard for the impact she has on others with her volatile expression of emotion. She is moody, unpredictable, and difficult to work with. In terms of her leadership development Sylvanna has two choices: If she gains some self-awareness of the impact she is having and wants to have a more positive impact because she values and respects her colleagues, she can develop the skill to express her feelings more positively and control her emotional outbursts. If she really doesn't care about the impact she has, she will continue with her current behavior, but will certainly spend more time and effort than she would like replacing team members who don't want to work with her.

If expressing feelings is a behavior that you currently don't use, I recommend that you give it a try. Start in easy situations where you know you have trust and credibility and work up to more difficult situations where there is less certainty. Try using the following structure to ensure that you are addressing the other person's behavior without getting emotional.

"I feel (the emotion you are feeling) about (the situation) because (the behavior in the other person that you hope to reinforce or change)."

Examples

"I feel excited (emotion) about the prospect of working with you on this project (situation) because you have been so involving and collaborative (behaviors you want to reinforce)."

"I am worried (emotion) about you working with our most important client (situation) because, on our last project, you missed agreed-upon deadlines (behavior that you want to change)."

It is important when using this structure that you also pay attention to your voice and body. If, for example, you say you are delighted, it would be helpful to look and sound delighted. If you say you are angry, it is important to name the emotion with a serious, calm, even voice—without actually getting angry.

Behavior #7: Stating what you want

Of all of the positive influencing behaviors, "stating what you want" is probably the least socially acceptable for women. Explicit messages such as "nice girls don't ask," "I want doesn't get," and being labeled "pushy" when they do say what they want, reinforces the implicit messages women have grown up with: It is unattractive and unfeminine to push themselves forward in this way.

Like most women, I have first-hand experience of this social stereotype. As a young, assertive manager in my early thirties, working in the male-dominated financial services industry, I remember chatting with a C-level executive who said, "Let's face it, Lynn, you're really a man in woman's clothing." He was referring to my lack of inhibition about stating what I wanted. It was one of many messages I received throughout my career in that organization that this was an unattractive trait that I really should do something about.

Stating expectations cleanly and clearly is one behavioral component of good leadership. A common complaint from people in organizations is that their manager is often not clear on exactly what she wants. If leaders are to lead effectively, they have to be clear about where they want to go and what it is likely to take to get there. However, social stereotypes imply that it is unladylike or unfeminine for women to state what they want and they are often penalized for doing so by attacks on their femininity. In Chapter Two we saw that this was one of the obstacles encountered by Hillary Clinton in her campaign for the United States Democratic presidential nomination in 2008. When she was being clear and assertive, stating what she wanted for the Democratic Party and for the country, she was labeled "grating" and "aggressive" and "trying too hard to be the smartest girl in the room."[74]

You might be forgiven at this stage for thinking that stating expectations is a behavior that you want nothing to do with; after all, it looks like a lose-lose situation for women. However, avoiding this behavior will not only make you a less-effective leader, it will put you at a disadvantage when it comes to competing with men for positions of leadership and for parity of remuneration.[75]

Knowing about this social stereotype, many women find indirect ways of saying what they want. Sometimes this works, but often it feels manipulative and leaves people unclear about where they stand and what is required. All good female leaders that I have worked with have been able to state what they want in a clean, clear, and nonaggressive way. Combined with skillful use of listening, asking good questions, finding common ground, and disclosing, these women manage to walk the fine line between assertion and aggression and demonstrate good leadership.

The behavior itself is very simple and is made up of two components:

1. Be clear in your own mind about what you want.

2. Make a short, clear statement of what you want, need or expect—*without embellishing it with reasons.*

Being clear in your own mind about what you want is crucial because, if you are unclear, you are likely to ramble while you work it out. This takes the power away from the behavior and makes you sound (quite rightly) like you don't really know what you want. Get clarity about the outcome you want before using this behavior.

Don't add reasons to support what you want when using this behavior. If you add reasons to your short, clear statement, you are encouraging a discussion. That might be appropriate in another situation, but not this one. A clear statement of expectation, unembellished with reasons, indicates that you are less open to debate and you are serious about what you want. (This, by the way, is a behavior that we were all very good at when we were children: "I want an ice cream." "I want to watch television." "I want Daddy." "I want to stay out as late as my friends.") Here are some examples of what it looks like in a more adult context:

"I would appreciate it if you could help me with this presentation."

"I would like you to give me a progress update at the end of each week."

"I need the report on my desk the day before the meeting."

"I want you to support my application for this job at the talent review meeting."

"I expect you to work closely together and present a joint proposal."

"I insist that you leave me alone."

You will notice that the words get stronger, moving from "I would appreciate" to "I insist." It is important to vary the strength of your message appropriately to the situation and to the person you are influencing. If you are always strongly stating what you want, need or expect you are likely to be seen as aggressive. Conversely, if you are always lightly stating what you would appreciate or what you would like, you may have trouble being taken seriously in situations where a stronger push is required. If you are building good relationships at work, it is likely that you would only need to work at the extreme of "I insist" on very rare occasions.

Tips on walking the fine line between assertion and aggression

Skillful use of this behavior will help you state what you want and avoid being labeled a "bully broad" or a "bitch." Try the following when practicing this behavior:

1. Ensure that you have worked out what it is you want and check that what you are asking for is reasonable.

2. Pay close attention to how you use your voice. It needs to be calm and firm, with a confidence that you expect to get what you are reasonably asking for.

3. Make good eye contact with the person you are influencing, without staring them down.

4. Show genuine recognition and empathy for the other person's position, if this is appropriate. For example, "I know you are very busy, but I do need this by the end of the day."

5. Combine "stating what you want" with the pull behaviors of listening, asking good questions, finding common ground, and disclosing. Flexing between positive push and pull behaviors will enable you to impact assertively and responsively, rather than aggressively and passively.

In reality, no matter how skillful you are with this behavior, some people will still experience you as "pushy" because you are confronting the stereotype of how women should behave. It is still the case that when men say what they want they are seen as assertive, but when women use the same behavior they are experienced as bossy. I recommend that you give yourself the best chance possible by developing your ability to state what you want in an assertive rather than an aggressive way, but at the same time understand that you might still be labeled "a pushy woman." Attitudes are changing toward women leaders, but they are not there yet. As Hillary Clinton stated, "I think that the world is only beginning to recognize that women should be permitted the same range of leadership styles that we permit men."[76] One certainty is that you can't lead effectively without the ability to clearly state your expectations, so it's a good idea to practice and improve your skill at saying what you want and learn what it takes to walk the fine line between impacting assertively and aggressively in your organization.

Behavior #8: Incentives and consequences

Incentives and consequences sound dangerously like bribes and threats—behaviors most of us would consider negative and not want anything to do with. Remember, all of the influencing behaviors can be used positively to do well or negatively to do harm. Used well, incentives and consequences can negotiate an agreed outcome and give others more information upon which to make decisions.

Example

Liz was leading a consulting project and wanted her colleague, Lynn, to be a part of the team. All team members needed to be proficient at working together at a distance using specific computer technology. Lynn avoided communicating with her colleagues via computer whenever possible, which was causing delays and frustrations. Liz tried to influence Lynn with logical reasoning, giving her good reasons why the team needed her to improve her computer skills. Lynn agreed with the logic, but did not change her behavior. Liz tried to influence Lynn one more time, expressing her frustration and stating clearly that she needed Lynn to learn to use the same technology as the rest of the team. Once again, Lynn agreed, but did not significantly change her behavior. In a final attempt to keep Lynn on the team, Liz decided to use incentives and pressures—here's what it looked like:

"Lynn, I want you to learn how the project management technology works, then use it to communicate on a daily basis with the rest of the team. I need you to do this by the end of the month (stating clear expectations). If you do this, I will spend some time helping you learn the technology (incentive). If you don't do this I won't include you in any of my future projects (consequence)."

Liz doesn't have any positional power with Lynn and, therefore, doesn't have the option of simply ordering her to comply with what the team needs. She tries to influence her using logical reasoning and expressing her feelings, but neither succeeds in getting Lynn to change her ways. Liz could have decided to give up at this stage and simply not invite Lynn to work with her on future projects. Instead, she made one final attempt to influence by using incentives and pressures. The incentive (to help Lynn learn to use the technology) made it easier for Lynn to do what Liz needed and helping Lynn was something that Liz was able and willing to do. In this particular situation, the consequence had the biggest influence on Lynn because she liked working with Liz and very much wanted to be included in her future projects.

This example highlights the importance of using incentives and consequences that are appropriate and meaningful to the person we are trying to influence. Using a consequence in this way might be construed as a threat. In fact, Liz had the option of simply not including Lynn in future projects, leaving Lynn guessing about why she never gets to work with Liz anymore. Instead, Liz gives Lynn the information she needs to make an informed choice about whether or not to change her behavior—"use the technology or I won' be inviting you onto any more of my projects." It's more helpful to Lynn to have the consequences of her behavior made clear than to have

Liz carry out the consequence without giving Lynn a last chance to comply. In this situation, Lynn did what was required of her because her desire to work with Liz was greater than her discomfort in learning to use the new technology.

Incentives and consequences are used in conjunction with stating expectations. Often, when we state our expectations clearly and those expectations are reasonable, others are happy to comply. In situations where we meet resistance it might be appropriate to use incentives and, as a last resort, consequences.

It is appropriate to use an incentive when we are asking the other person to do something that they don't necessarily have to do; for example, staying late to finish some work, doing something outside of their normal role, or putting their own needs aside to help others. It is not appropriate to use incentives for things that people should be doing as part of their job; for example, turning up on time, collaborating with colleagues, and meeting agreed-upon deadlines.

It is appropriate to use consequences to influence a situation: first, when we are prepared to carry out the consequence; and second, when it would be only fair to let the other person know the consequences of their actions, so that the person has the opportunity to make an informed choice. Incentives and consequences are useful influencing behaviors but are likely to be only needed occasionally if we are using the other behaviors well.

Summary

Becoming highly proficient—in not only using these eight distinct influencing behaviors, but also in learning how to combine the behaviors to achieve tactical and strategic results—will help you to demonstrate good leadership and navigate the *unwritten rules* and stereotypes of today's organizations. Learning how to do this takes guidance and practice and, as such, I recommend that you not only experiment with the behaviors described in this chapter, but that you also attend a workshop where you will get feedback to improve your skill level and impact. Behavioral change is more effectively realized through experiential rather than theoretical learning experiences. For further information on workshops for women leaders go to www.unwrittenrulesthebook.com.

Chapter Six

Building Strategic Professional Relationships

> **UNWRITTEN RULE:**
> ### *Senior leaders promote themselves*
> **This means:**
> - They build relationships with people who can support their career progression.

In Chapter Two we identified the *unwritten rules* that determine leadership behavior in today's organizations. We recognized that, in order for leaders to progress their careers within their organization or profession, they must speak confidently about their accomplishments to people who can positively influence their career and build relationships with people who can support their career progression. This is commonly known as "networking" and many women don't like doing it.

Comments from some of my coaching clients:

"Relationships should develop naturally. It's like Internet-dating; you shouldn't have to plan relationships."

"People who network contact you only when they want something. There's one woman I've only heard from twice—both times because she was looking for a new job."

"Networking events are awful. They are full of people thrusting business cards into your hand while looking over your shoulder for someone who might be more useful."

"I don't have the time or the energy to network. At the end of the day, all I want to do is get home to see my kids before they go to bed. The last thing I want is a business dinner or networking event."

In the light of such comments, it may be helpful to clarify what building strategic professional relationships are *not* about. They are not about exchanging business cards, working a room, having unproductive lunch or coffee meetings, sucking up to important people or manipulating others for your own benefit. If you want tips on how to connect with others and how to work a room, there are plenty of books available to help with this. What we are talking about here is **building strategic business relationships as a core leadership competency.** Essentially, it is the ability to identify, build, and leverage purposeful relationships with individuals of diverse backgrounds both inside and outside of your organization. They are relationships that will broaden your thinking and expose you to different experiences. They will also enable you to contribute to the success of others and support your ability to influence strategically both for your own benefit and for the success of your team and organization.

Why bother?

As a leader you need access to different sources of information from which you can gain new insight and make intelligent decisions. You also need to use your experience and insight to influence across diverse groups internal and external to your organization. It is not possible to do this if your professional relationships are predominantly limited to your functional group within the company you work for. Building relationships is a business enabler that helps you to achieve your goals and maximize individual, team and organizational performance.

Many women I have coached have become successful through their ability to drive tasks to successful completion—they think well and reliably get things done to a high standard. What often hinders their career progression and their ability to influence more widely is their lack of motivation or ability (in most cases it is motivation rather than ability) to build and leverage strategic professional relationships. Although most agree that networking is important, many women don't seem to know how to successfully build a diverse relationship network and fail to recognize the importance and opportunities afforded by developing this as a core leadership competency. If you fall into this category, your mental conception of building strategic professional relationships needs to move from a "nice to do if I had the time" to an "essential leadership attribute I need to master," particularly if you have aspirations for promotion to higher corporate positions.

Building strategic professional relationships enables you to:

- Develop your leadership capacity by accessing diverse perspectives and relevant information from which you can gain new insights and make intelligent decisions.

- Influence successfully within your industry/profession and across your organization.

- Support others within your network of relationships.

- Get the support you need to be even more successful in your current role.

- Influence your career progression.

- Gain energy and stimulation from interesting people.

Taking this seriously as a core leadership competency can make the difference between being a good leader who is stuck in your current role, to an excellent leader who is going places; between being a member of a profession, and a respected leader of that profession; between being a person whose sphere of influence is small, to a leader who is known and respected by many; and between being a person who thinks and acts strategically to manage your career, and someone who reacts to career opportunities if and when they come along.

Orientation

The first step is to decide if you believe in the value of building professional relationships and if you are going to take it seriously as a leadership competency. Unless you position relationship building as part of your role as a leader, it will always be a task on your to-do list that gets preceded by other tasks. Building strategic professional relationships is not a task; it is an orientation—a way that you think and conduct yourself in your work environment. It helps if you reframe it from yet another task on your already long to-do list, to an integrated behavior that is part of your leadership brand (a brand being what you are known for). Investing in building professional relationships is something that you do all of the time, not as a special event when you need something from others.

If your experience of networking has so far been unproductive lunches, tedious networking events and people who contact you only when they want something, it is likely that you will be skeptical (and quite rightly) about devoting time and energy in this way. If you have always thought of networking as trying to use people for your own gain, or building relationships as something that should happen naturally without thinking about it, you are likely to question whether this fits with your values. I encourage you to relax those views and opinions, at least for the rest of this chapter, and think about whether a different approach could work for you.

Values

If you value the professional relationships that you build only for what they can do for you, you are unlikely to be successful or to enjoy building professional relationships. None of us likes to be used by others and we are unlikely to form a sustainable professional network if we value only a "what's in it for us" approach. Those who create successful business networks come from a values base of "what can

I do for others" and are prepared to invest in relationships without needing anything in return.

The dos and don'ts of building a network of strategic professional relationships

A reactive response to relationship building goes something like: "I will set aside five hours per week to network." This doesn't usually work because you are creating a task out of a perceived need. As soon as more immediate needs come along, this task drops off the end of your to-do list. A more strategic approach is to create a diverse network of relationships as a way of life. If you are having trouble imagining what this looks like, here are some tips from people who are good at it:

Be open and available

Establishing meaningful contact with other people requires some effort on your part. It's very easy, particularly when you lead a very full and busy life, to shut yourself off from those around you. I am all in favor of downtime in order to rest and recuperate, but if you make a habit of deliberately ignoring people around you who you don't know, you are likely to be cutting yourself off from establishing potentially interesting and diverse relationships.

Sharon is now a senior executive in a Fortune 500 company. She learned her lesson about making herself open and available to establishing new contacts early in her career:

"I was on a plane in one of those business class seats that have you facing your fellow passenger with a screen that you can put up between you, if you want privacy. While waiting for takeoff, I couldn't fail to notice that the guy in the seat opposite was trying to engage my attention. He tried to make eye contact, asked me questions, made jokey comments, and generally persisted, even though I buried my head in a book, trying to make it obvious that I did not want to engage with him. Finally, I got so fed up with him that I was quite rude. He seemed to take this as a further challenge and, in a very good-natured way, ignored my rudeness and still tried to pleasantly engage me in conversation. So I gave up, put down my book and asked him who he was and what he did. Much to my shock and horror, he turned out to be one of our most important clients. I introduced myself and asked him how rude he thought I had been. "Pretty rude," he said, but luckily for me he made a joke of it. We had a fantastic discussion and I developed a really important business contact. And I even enjoyed his company. This was a great lesson for me early in my career. Since then I have never made the same mistake again."

Invest in others

Find ways to invest in and become an asset to others. Unfortunately, some people think of building relationships only when they need something, which then has the impact of being insincere and self-serving (probably because it is). Most good networkers that I know spend more time helping others than intentionally seeking personal benefit. They invest in people in various ways: by connecting people through introductions and referrals; by helping others to think things through; by giving helpful advice; by giving their time to help in some way (like the many people who gave their time to be interviewed for this book); by extending invitations to events where the other person can make interesting connections and learn something new; and by spreading the good word about a person or their work.

It is possible to become thoughtful and creative about how you invest in others. When I moved from the United Kingdom to live in Canada, I was lucky enough to be introduced to Deborah Hinton, a woman who makes it her business to invest in others. Not only did she introduce me to a fabulous network of professional business-women, she also threw a party at her apartment under the theme of "Who is Lynn Harris?" specifically to help me get started in a new city. Building relationships through the connections I initially made from Deborah resulted in both friendships and introductions into local organizations and formed the basis on the consulting work I have in Montreal today. Deborah is known for the energy she puts into relationship building and uses it as the foundation of her communications consulting practice (www.hintonandco.com).

Sue Baker, a management consultant based in the United Kingdom, also continues to build her business through investing in others.

"Many years ago when I was head of Organizational Development for a large U.K. company, I was able to help someone who to this day continues to repay that investment. I was leading a working group as part of a huge culture change program when I became aware of Chris, who had been parachuted into Group Head Office with the difficult remit of aligning performance management processes across different parts of the organization. It was a big task because each division was doing its own thing and, at that stage, Chris didn't know his way around. I invited him to join my working group because I could see he was struggling. I introduced him to people, shared materials and information, and generally helped in whatever way I could. I didn't do this in order to get anything in return; it's just the way that I operate. After I left the company I kept in touch with Chris by e-mail and, when he was considering moving jobs, he contacted me for advice and I was glad to help.

Since then I have started my own consulting practice and Chris has moved to different organizations, each time bringing me in as a consultant. I have developed an enormous amount of business through introductions from

> Chris and this absolutely would never have happened if I hadn't originally reached out and invested time and energy to help him. It wasn't my original motivation for helping him, but I do believe that if we invest in others it will come back to us at some point."

The orientation of people like Deborah and Sue, who both develop business through building successful relationship networks, is: Ask not what your network can do for you, but what you can do for your network.

Dig your well before you are thirsty

This is the title of a networking book by Harvey Mackay.[77] The message is that you need to build your network of relationships through investing in others long before you need help or support from the people in that network. This might sound calculating and transactional, but it is true that most of us are reciprocal by nature. If I have an established relationship with someone I like and respect who has supported me in some way in the past, I am more inclined to go out of my way to help them when they need it. In fact, I am likely to be positively eager to grab an opportunity to return the favor. This is not to say that you invest in others with the expectation that they should reciprocate. It simply means that if you have helped and supported other people you are likely to find it much easier to ask for and get help when you need some support yourself. Conversely, if you initiate contact with people only when you want something, you will quite rightly be viewed as self-serving, and when you need support you will have a much harder time getting it.

> "I started building my network when I arrived in Montreal many years ago and my career wouldn't be where it is today if I hadn't developed and maintained these relationships. A relationship network is a powerful tool, if it is used well. What I find is that many people go into networking mode only when they lose their job and then don't maintain those

relationships once they have secured a new position. In my mind, developing and maintaining a relationship network is something that you do all of the time and it's a two-way street; it's essential to give to others as well as receive their support."

Katya Laviolette. VP, People & Culture, CBC/Radio Canada

Do it all the time

We all have the opportunity to build relationships every day, both inside and outside of our organizations. Unfortunately, we tend to rush through our workweek with our head down, buried in our to-do list. How often do you contact a friend or colleague, just to find out how they are? When was the last time you stopped to talk to other parents at the day care; engaged your fellow passenger in conversation on the airplane; or sat at the same table with someone you didn't know in the company restaurant? A recent trip reminded me of the opportunities that are often right in front of us every day for meeting interesting and stimulating people:

It was a late flight from New York to Montreal; I was tired after a couple of days' executive coaching at a large pharmaceutical company; the plane was small and cramped and we were in a long line up for takeoff, which meant at least an hour delay. I was tempted to bury my nose into my book, but also aware of my fellow passenger crammed into the seat next to me. I asked myself, could I be bothered to initiate conversation with this stranger? What if he turns out to be really boring and I'm stuck listening to him for the next couple of hours? This is the internal conversation I often have with myself on airplanes; sometimes the book wins and sometimes I meet interesting people who I would never normally get the chance to talk with in my everyday work.

His name was Daniel Myssyk and we talked nonstop through the flight delay and all of the way back to Montreal. Daniel is the artistic director and conductor of Appassionata, a Montreal-based orchestra. Our conversation included discovering mutual friends, talking about our children, discussing music, and discovering that I had actually been to one of Daniel's performances when I first moved to Montreal. He was charming and interesting. The long and tedious flight passed quickly and concluded with an invitation from Daniel to attend a future concert. Once again I proved to myself how satisfying it is when I take the opportunity to meet someone new, rather than staying within my own little world and ignoring the people around me.

In addition to recognizing and taking opportunities to talk to new people every day, it is also a good idea to build time into your schedule every week or month where you create opportunities to build new relationships or strengthen existing ones. Invite interesting people for breakfast, lunch, or coffee; arrange to travel to a meeting with someone you want to get to know better; forward a relevant article to people in your network; be the catalyst for getting a stimulating group of people together to discuss something of mutual benefit; renew established relationships by keeping in touch by phone or e-mail just to find out how the other person is doing, and so on. Establishing new relationships and staying in touch with interesting people becomes enjoyable rather than a chore if we just lift our heads from our checklists long enough to look around and realize that life is about more than getting things done.

Be interested and interesting

Building a network of relationships requires mutual connection where both parties are stimulated by the interaction. This is easy to establish if you show genuine curiosity about other people—what are they thinking, doing, creating and struggling with? What is going on in their world and is there any way that you can provide useful information, insight or connections? Fruitful conversations result from getting off your own agenda and showing interest in others by asking good questions. If this is not a skill that comes naturally to you, go back to Chapter Five and remind yourself of the strategic influencing skills, particularly the pull behaviors of listening, asking good questions, finding common ground and disclosing. These are the primary behaviors that you need to show interest and make meaningful contact with others. Practicing these behaviors with new people will not only improve your interpersonal skills, it will also result in stimulating conversation and new relationships that you may want to add to your personal or professional network.

Don't be afraid to talk about yourself

If building a network of relationships is about mutual connections, it's not enough to just show interest in others. Women have a reputation for putting others' needs and interests before their own, which might be an admirable quality but will not result in mutual connections and a network of mutually beneficial relationships.

If you look back again at the behavior of disclosing in Chapter Five will see that it is about giving the other person helpful information, in this case about yourself. Some women I coach have a problem talking about themselves because they don't think other people will find them interesting. My advice is to let others be the judge of this rather than you making up their mind for them. If people don't find you interesting, they will usually politely disengage, but if you never give others the chance to get to know you it will be very hard for them to form a real connection with you and include you in their network.

In addition to listening and asking good questions, be prepared to disclose information about you, your ideas, your work, your interests and your aspirations. Ideally you should leave the conversation both knowing more about each other, rather than just you knowing more about them.

Be a Connector

In his book *The Tipping Point,* Malcolm Gladwell[78] identifies people he calls Connectors. Connectors know lots of people and have an ability to bring individuals and groups together. You probably know at least one Connector yourself—someone who seems to know everyone through an extraordinary knack for making friends and acquaintances. They connect people, things and ideas and sometimes make creative referrals that others wouldn't have thought of.

For obvious reasons, it is extremely beneficial to have Connectors as part of your network of relationships—they are not only invaluable when you are looking for ideas, help or support, but they are also easy to ask because they enjoy putting people together. You might also start behaving like a Connector yourself as a way of investing in others. Purposefully opening yourself up to building relationships, then introducing or referring people to each other is one of the ways you can create your personal brand as a connector and a person known for leveraging her network to help others.

Attend and speak at conferences

Attending conferences is one of the best ways I know of meeting interesting people and being exposed to stimulating ideas and conversation. What's even better is to be one of the speakers at a conference yourself because then other people make the approach and want to talk to you. This really hit home to me when I spoke at the 2008 conference for The International Alliance for Women (TIAW). It had been a while since I attended a conference and even longer since I had spoken at one. The presentation went well and for the next two days of the conference I had a steady stream of people wanting to talk with me over lunch or cocktails. I met several very interesting women, increased my knowledge in areas that I didn't even know I was interested in, such as angel investing and micro enterprise, and have since been in contact with a few of these women who have now become part of my relationship network. The whole experience was both stimulating and enjoyable and as a result my commitment is renewed to investing more time and energy to speak at other conferences.

If you are reasonably comfortable speaking to groups, you could start by telling people at work, in your professional organization or in your current network that you would be interested to speak at a conference on your area of expertise. If you would rather cut out your tongue than speak to a large audience it would still be a good investment of your time to attend at least one conference per year where you think you will hear interesting speakers and develop new professional relationships. Attending a conference is one of those activities that seem like a lot of effort and expense when we are thinking about it, but once achieved we inevitably find it stimulating and worthwhile.

Join professional networks

Many people ask me if it is worthwhile to join professional networks. My answer is yes, but be selective. There's little point in collecting networks if you don't use them because you either don't know how to or because they are not relevant to you. A good example of this would be professional online networks such as LinkedIn and Plaxo. Most people I know accept invitations from others to join their online network, derive some satisfaction from seeing their number of contacts grow, but don't really know what to do with the network once they have it. Online business networks have been successfully established with the specific intention of connecting experienced professionals from around the world. LinkedIn, for example, represents 170 industries and two hundred countries. The idea is that you can find, be introduced to, and collaborate with professionals that you can work with to accomplish your goals. I have successfully used LinkedIn to reconnect with people I had lost touch with, keep track of and in contact with the many people I know around the world, gain introductions to people I wanted to meet, get recommendations from people I have worked with and as a marketing tool for the work I do. My LinkedIn network was also an invaluable resource when I was looking for women to interview for this book.

It's very easy to set up and manage an online network. You simply create a profile that summarizes your professional expertise and accomplishments and start connecting with others that you know through the search facility. I strongly recommend that, if you are going to use an online resource such as this, you take the time to create a full and accurate profile of yourself. It is likely that many people will look at your profile and one that is incomplete or done half-heartedly creates a poor impression. Online networks do not replace the more valuable face-to-face contact but they are a useful addition if used well.

It is also worth considering other types of networks, such as those that may exist within your own organization and external networks that are specific to your profession or your particular interests. Most large organizations have internal networks that are used for advocacy of important issues, personal and professional development, mutual support, recruitment and retention, to promote the advancement of diversity and to provide networking opportunities. If you are already a senior leader in an organization, they also provide a vehicle for role modeling and investing in the careers of others.

Additionally, there are worldwide women's networks, such as The International Alliance for Women (TIAW), The European Professional Women's network (EuropeanPWN) and the International Women's Forum (IWF) that provide excellent annual conferences, a vehicle to connect with women from other cultures and up to date research on issues pertinent to professional women. As someone who had initial reticence about becoming involved with women's networks, I can honestly say that I have found the ones I have joined to be enjoyable, stimulating and informative. They have certainly enabled me to get to know some fabulous professional women and I come away from meetings and conferences energized from the contact with a diverse group of people. It should not be forgotten, however, that we need to build professional relationships with both women and men; therefore, women's networks should form only part of our relationship building activity.

Follow through

It is only possible to build a network of professional relationships if you make opportunities to reconnect and stay in touch with people. This can seem like an impossible task when you are busy and know so many people. Karim Salabi, VP Marketing, Media and Entertainment Solutions at Autodesk, builds and maintains an extensive professional network through his strength of keeping in touch with people. Karim has a big job, travels frequently and is a devoted family man and yet still manages to make time to connect with many people, and so I asked him how he does it?

"I see networking as more of a reward than a chore. I'm always motivated to make time for relationship building, because I like the friends and colleagues I have in my network and I gain positive energy from seeing or speaking to them. For example, when you asked to interview me for this book, I had an incredibly full week ahead of me, but I thought how great it would be to spend an hour with you over breakfast on a Thursday morning.

In terms of keeping in touch with my network, I have a few strategies that work well for me: if I'm not traveling I'll make a point of arranging breakfast with at least one person during the week. I often arrange these breakfast meetings on a Thursday or Friday because that's the point in the week when I benefit from some positive stimulation outside of my workplace. I am the one who usually initiates the contact and so I have control over who I keep in contact with. When I hear of job opportunities, I circulate them to people who might be interested. This shows others that I am thinking of them and they are always appreciative, particularly because they know how busy I am. I use my one hour commute home each evening to phone contacts who I know will still be in their office at that time, just to catch up with them and see how they are. I send Christmas cards the old fashioned way, with a personalized message, which stands out because not many people do that with their business contacts these days. It takes me two weeks to write two hundred cards but it's worth it. I also keep a list of fifty–sixty people with the last date that I saw them for lunch or breakfast. I review this list about once per month and highlight anyone I haven't seen for a while to remind me to initiate contact."

Karim likens building a network of relationships to strategic planning:

"You don't just do strategic planning once a year; you do it every day because you never know when a good idea is going to pop into your head. It's the same with building relationships and networking; you do it every day as part of your day."

I have described here what I consider to be an authentic and value-based approach to building professional relationships. It is organic in its growth, rather than highly structured and organized—more of a way of life than a plan. If, however, you think that a more planned and structured approach to building a network would work better for you, I recommend David Nour's book, *Relationship Economics. Transform your most valuable business contacts into personal and professional success.*[79']

It is also important to recognize that a more structured and intentional approach is often needed for women to progress within today's organizations where leadership behavior is heavily influenced by the *unwritten rules*. In such circumstances, it is important to be intentional about relationship building within your organization, in addition to a more organic approach of building a broader network. To progress in your career, you do need to build relationships upwards and sideways, in addition to investing in the people who report to you.

Being a fabulous leader to your team is not enough if your boss's boss knows little or nothing about you, and if your cross-functional colleagues only know you as an e-mail address. You are not likely to get the promotion you want if half the people on the selection committee don't know who you are.

It's pretty simple to take a planned approach to building relationships, if you can define the specific outcomes that you want. If you have a specific aspiration in your organization, for example, to position yourself as the natural successor to your boss, or to be invited to speak at the next company conference, or just about anything else that requires the input of other people in your organization, go to www.unwrittenrulesthebook.com for a simple structured process that will help you plan your approach.

The don'ts of building professional relationships

The don'ts are pretty obvious, but I'll mention them anyway just to hammer home the points:

- Don't confuse collecting business cards and endless lunches with building a network of professional relationships.

- Don't assume that senior people will be more helpful to you; every senior person was a junior person once.

- Don't confine yourself to people just like you; aim for diversity.

- Don't think short term—what can this person do for me now.

- Don't contact people only when you want something.

- Don't make the mistake of thinking that building a network of professional relationships is optional or a nice to have if you want to succeed within the structure of the *unwritten rules*.

Creating a personal support network

In addition to building a robust professional network, it is also important to give some attention to a *personal* support network. If you are in or working toward a senior leadership position, you will likely already be experiencing the *unwritten rule* of "Available anytime, anywhere":

UNWRITTEN RULE:

Senior leaders are available anytime and anywhere

This means:
- They are always available. Full-time work is the norm and part-time work is out of the question or career limiting.
- They must be physically present in an office for ten or more hours per day, with little or no flexible working or working from home.
- They travel extensively as part of their job.

The only way to succeed within this *unwritten rule* is to establish a comprehensive personal support network, particularly if you have a family. In my experience, male leaders find this easier than female leaders and consequently reap the benefits. The reality is, more men have wives who take on the full-time roles of parent, housekeeper, social secretary, travel agent, cook and so on. We are seeing an increasing number of female leaders with partners who take on this support role, but it is still relatively unusual and you can't rely on your partner wanting to arrange their life in this way just to support you.

If you are to succeed within the *unwritten rule* of "Total availability" it is up to you to create a comprehensive personal support network. Many women I know struggle with this: they take on the primary childcare, housekeeping and social secretary roles for their family, in addition to the massive time and energy commitment of an organizational leadership role. They somehow feel uncomfortable with releasing control of family related activities and try to do too much themselves. It is also common that they feel resentment toward their partner (who also often has a demanding job) because he does not do more to help.

If you aspire to or are in an organizational leadership role that includes the *unwritten rule* of "Total availability" and you do not have a good personal support network outside of the workplace, I strongly recommend that you create one. If you are in a position to do so, spend some of your hard-earned money on professional childcare, a cleaner who visits as often as needed, and possibly even someone to shop and cook. I also recommend that you explore the possibilities of using a remote personal assistant. You probably have a business assistant at work. Why not have personal assistants outside of work? If your immediate reaction is, I couldn't possibly afford or manage this, think again.

If you have not read Tim Ferriss' book *The 4-hour work week*,[80] you might be surprised to discover that it is simple and affordable to outsource parts of your life, leaving you more time and energy to concentrate on activities you enjoy, such as spending time with your children or enjoying some physical exercise. By using a remote assistant, it is possible to outsource such things as: arranging trips and vacations, sending cards and gifts, arranging household repairs, liaising with your children's school, finding a parking slot for your car in a city you are going to visit, researching the best play in town and booking tickets, organizing parties, finding and managing caterers, cleaning up your personal accounts, and just about anything it is possible to delegate. The cost is relatively low, usually somewhere between $5–$20 per hour and you can manage everything remotely from your computer or PDA. If this sounds like an interesting idea, check out Ferriss' book (Chapter Eight on outsourcing your life gives lots of advice on how to manage a remote assistant) and take a look at the following sites:

www.elance.com

www.b2kcorp.com

www.assistu.com

www.yourvirtualresource.com

www.ivaa.org

www.yourmaninindia.com

However you manage it, the message here is that you are not super-woman, you can't have and do it all, and establishing personal and professional support networks are essential in helping you to achieve what is most important to you.

Chapter Seven

Mentoring and Coaching

In the same way that building a network of professional relationships is an essential leadership competency, building mentoring relation-ships is a mandatory requirement for guiding and supporting your career progression. In an organizational world where the *unwritten rules* create a more difficult environment for women who aspire to higher levels of leadership, the sponsorship of more experienced and well-connected people is, at the very least, extremely helpful.

Mentoring programs have become popular vehicles for organizations to attempt to groom their next generation of leaders. Unfortunately, many of these programs do not live up to their potential because senior leaders are often coerced into becoming mentors with little or no regard for their aptitude to do the job, combined with minimal development on how to be a good mentor; and the people being mentored (who, for lack of a better term, we will call "mentees") are often equally unprepared to set up and make the most of the relationship. The intention is good on both sides, but the execution doesn't always get the results that such opportunities afford.

This is why you need to take charge of creating, developing and maintaining good mentoring relationships with people who can guide and support your career development, particularly if your organization has no mentoring program or one that is poorly set up and managed. If you haven't already got at least one good mentoring relationship, don't be passive and wait for your organization to establish it for you; it's too important. It's not about being chosen to be a mentee, but rather about developing a mentoring mentality and taking accountability for making it happen. This chapter will help you to do just that.

The mentoring relationship

Mentoring has a clear purpose. It is a developmental relationship that enables a more experienced mentor to guide a less experienced partner or mentee. "More experienced" doesn't have to mean older or even more senior in the organization; it may simply mean someone who has experience or expertise that you don't have and that you think will be helpful. This means that you can develop fruitful mentoring relationships both within and outside of your organization, and with peers, as well as more senior people. You can even benefit from the experience of a mentor who is junior to you, something known as "reverse mentoring." In 1999, then GE chief executive officer Jack Welch famously established a reverse mentoring initiative for himself and other top executives, so they could learn from the younger, tech savvy generation below them. The key difference between any mentoring relationship and the professional networking relationships we explored in Chapter Six is that mentoring relationships have a specific developmental purpose—they are established with the expressed purpose of guiding and supporting the development of the mentee.

The many roles of mentors

To be able to identify people who might act as good mentors for you, it is helpful to understand the differing roles that mentors can fulfill.

No mentor should be expected to play all of these roles, but you do need to think about what you are looking for before selecting and approaching someone to be your mentor.

Counselor and Thinking Partner

In this role, the mentor acts as a sounding board to help you address work-related issues. He or she can help you navigate the organizational culture, plan and decide career choices, strategize to support achievement of your career goals and offer advice from their own professional experience.

Coach or Advisor

In a coaching or advisory role, the mentor gives candid feedback and advice, helps you to clarify performance goals and development needs, reviews your development plan on a regular basis, and shares their experience and expertise.

Role Model

Many successful men and women have reported the positive benefits of observing others who they admire in influencing their own leadership behavior. A mentor who acts as a positive role model is likely to be known as a good leader who demonstrates organizational political awareness, behaves authentically and honestly, does what he or she commits to, can be trusted to maintain confidentiality, and leads by example.

Advocate or Champion

Sometimes (although it should not be expected), mentors can be your advocate or champion. In this role the mentor might sponsor you for key projects and development opportunities, support your application for promotion, help you to gain exposure by introducing you to members of their professional network, and arrange for you to participate in highly visible activities within or outside of your organization.

The first step in identifying possible mentoring candidates is to review these roles and decide what you are looking for in a mentor. This should help you to identify people to approach. Even if you work in a company with an established mentoring program where you are assigned a mentor, I still encourage you to go through this thinking process. It is always possible to influence who might be assigned to mentor you, but to do this, you have to first know what type of support you are looking for. It is also possible to work with more than one mentor. You might therefore work with the mentor assigned to you and approach an additional mentor of your choice.

Internal or external mentors?

Ideally, you should have both a mentor who is part of your company who can help you to navigate within your organization and an external mentor who can take a more impartial and independent view, as well as introducing you to external networks. As we saw in the previous chapter, it is a mistake to restrict your professional relationship building to your current organization—ask anyone who has recently lost his or her job!

Male or female mentors?

Many women have asked me if it would be better for them to work with a male or female mentor. The answer is entirely dependent on your purpose for wanting a mentoring relationship. If, for example, you would like to understand how women succeed to higher levels of leadership within your organization you are likely to be looking for a senior woman executive within your company. If you are looking for help to navigate the politics of your company culture and most or all of your senior leadership are men, you might be better off approaching one of the male executives. Or, if you simply want to benefit from the wisdom of a role model, gender may not even come into the decision. Think about your purpose for working with a mentor before addressing any questions of whether your mentor should be internal or external, male or female.

Formal versus informal mentoring

There's nothing wrong with informal mentoring relationships where you simply get together on mutually convenient occasions. Mentoring works best, however, when it is structured and formal. You and your mentor are busy people and you will only get the best from a mentoring relationship if it is formalized so that you both make time for each other and treat your time together as important. If you don't do this, you are likely to find that meetings are frequently postponed and the relationship fails. The first step in establishing a formalized mentoring relationship is to identify potential mentors.

How to identify the right mentor for you

Completing steps one to four below will increase your chances of getting a good match in your mentoring relationships:

1. Review the "many roles of mentors" above and decide what you are looking for from an internal and an external mentor. You should be able to define the purpose of the mentoring relationship in each case. This should not include expecting a mentor to be your advocate or champion, even though this is one of the described roles. It is the mentor's choice whether or not to take on this role and should not be an expectation on your part.

2. Write a short description of why you want a mentor and the purpose of the mentoring relationship. For example, "I want a mentor to give me guidance and advice on how to increase my presence and profile within the company," or "I want a mentor to help me to understand how I can build a better network of professional relationships outside of my organization," or "I need a mentor to support my professional development of understanding the financial aspects of our business."

3. Make two short lists: one of possible mentors inside your organization and one of possible external mentors. Do not restrict yourself to who you think would be interested or have the

time to mentor you. List your ideal mentors without making up their minds for them. Do not let geography act as a barrier to your thinking. Many successful mentoring relationships are conducted by phone as well as in person.

4. For each person on your list write down the attributes of the person that you think would make them a good mentor for you.

Example:

Purpose:

I want a mentor to help me to understand how I can build a better network of professional relationships outside of my organization.

Possible candidates:

Karl: He seems to know everyone and everyone seems to know him; he has a big job but still seems to find time to meet people and build a network; he is friendly, approachable and has a good reputation; he is well traveled and has worked in different companies around the world; and he has some knowledge of me, since we were both part of a previous project team.

Susan: I had a good relationship with her when she was my boss; she has achieved rapid promotion and I suspect it's partly because of who she knows, as well as because she is really good at her job; she is known for her support of other women; I want to stay on her radar because I'd love to work with her again in the future.

David: He has a customer-facing role and lots of contacts in our profession; he seems to generate most of his business through relationship building; rumor has it that he is in line to lead a major division in the near future, so he is also well thought of and well connected within and outside of the company; I don't know him, but my boss knows him well and could make an introduction.

Identifying potential mentors should be pretty straightforward, but if you are having trouble coming up with names because you currently have a very limited professional relationship network, I encourage you to ask for help. Talk to your boss, someone in human resources, friends, colleagues, or acquaintances who are well connected. Describe why you want to develop mentoring relationships, what you are ideally looking for in a mentor, and see if they are able to point you in the right direction.

Approaching a possible mentor

Once you have identified possible mentoring candidates, you are in a position to approach them—either directly or through an introduction, depending on whether or not you have an existing relationship with them. This is the stage at which some women fail to act because of a small, internal voice that says, "They probably won't have time," or "Why would they want to mentor me?" or "They are too important or too senior for me to approach," or other variations on the same theme. If you are the proud owner of just such a voice I strongly encourage you to recognize it for what it is—an imaginary fear—and simply ignore it. In reality, you have no idea whether or not the potential mentors you have identified will want to form such a relationship with you and it would be arrogant of you to make up their minds for them. The worst that can happen is that they will ignore you or politely say no. You can survive this level of rejection and, if you can't (which I very much doubt), save yourself some pain and step off the career advancement ladder right now.

How you approach a potential mentor is important because your initial impact will influence whether or not the person wants to devote time and energy to you. I recently coached a woman who complained that the person she wanted as a mentor had bluntly rejected her request. When I explored a little further, I discovered that she had been extremely vague about what she wanted from a mentor and, quite rightly, the senior executive in question told her to go away and think about why she was approaching him. It wasn't a great start.

Most people are flattered to be asked to become a mentor, especially if you tell them why you are asking them. This is not about sucking up to people; it is simply about stating clearly and concisely that you are interested in exploring the possibility of forming a mentoring relationship, why you want a mentor and why you are asking them.

For example:

"Lily, I'd like to spend half an hour with you to explore the possibility of a formal mentoring relationship. I want to work with a mentor because I have aspirations to become a senior leader in this company and I need some help navigating the politics and creating a development plan. The reason I'm asking you is that you are very successful and seem to be able to manage the politics and at the same time I admire your ability to stay true to yourself. Would you be open to talking about the possibility of a mentoring relationship with me, perhaps over a coffee sometime this week?"

This is just an example and I encourage you to use your own words, but, before doing so, be clear—first with yourself and then with your potential mentor—about what you want, why you want it, and, specifically, why you are asking them. If you are approaching someone through an intermediary, ensure the person making the introduction for you is also clear so that it is easy for him or her to recommend you.

Creating the mentoring relationship

Once someone has agreed to be your mentor, it is up to you to be a good partner or mentee. It needs both of you to create a good working relationship, but it is up to you to drive the logistics and the agenda. As a good mentee, it is your job to:

- Be proactive in scheduling a series of regular meetings and establish with your mentor the importance of these meetings and a willingness from both parties to try to reschedule as seldom as possible.

- Make agreements in the first meeting about how you will work together (go to www.unwrittenrulesthebook.com for specific suggestions on what to cover in your first meeting).

- Make good use of your mentor's time by setting an agenda for meetings or at least being clear about what you want to talk about.

- Ask for advice and feedback, then listen and ask good questions (rather than getting defensive and pushing back, if you don't like what you hear).

- Ask a lot of questions—you have two ears and one mouth, try to use them in that proportion.

- Be open with your mentor about your aspirations, your strengths, your weaknesses, and your successes and failures.

- Give feedback to your mentor about the impact of his or her mentoring—what is helpful and working for you; what is less helpful or getting in the way.

- Ask for feedback about the impact you are having on your mentor.

- Look for ways to build a reciprocal relationship—is there any way that you can return the favor and be of help to your mentor?

- Become a mentor yourself—there is nothing like being on the other side of the fence for helping you to understand how to get and give the best in a mentoring relationship.

Organizations, particularly large organizations, are challenging environments in which to navigate and succeed. If you aspire to positions of senior leadership within these environments, it is common sense, as well as good business practice, to seek the support of people who are more experienced. Developing good mentoring relationships should be part of your strategy for personal sustainability and career advancement. You would be crazy not to avail yourself of this available resource. In addition to a mentor, a further possible resource to support you in succeeding in your current role, as well as helping you to prepare for career progression, is an executive coach.

Executive coaching—It's all about you!

Executive coaching really is all about you. It's about targeted professional development to optimize your capability as a leader and manager. More managers and leaders are requesting coaching for themselves. The outdated negative connotation of coaching as a form of punishment for poor performance has been replaced by the realization that coaching can help an individual or group to build sustainable professional and personal skills, learn better, overcome challenges, reach demanding goals, and integrate leadership training.

If you've never experienced the benefits of good executive coaching here's how it works. To begin with, it helps to have some idea of the type of coaching that would be most helpful to you at this particular moment in your career. For example:

1. **Behavioral/Leadership coaching:** Coaching to change certain limiting behaviors or develop interpersonal skills that you need to become a more effective leader or team member; aligning your leadership behavior with your values; building more successful working relationships; strategic influencing skills; running effective meetings; and building and managing a successful team.

2. **Career/Life coaching:** Coaching to create the career and life that you really want; improving your decision making skills; examining personal, as well as professional, issues; living in

alignment with your values; and learning to integrate a fulfill-ing work/life balance.

3. **Strategy coaching:** Coaching leaders to establish the long-term vision and direction of their division or company; and acting as an unbiased sounding board for new ideas.

4. **Transition coaching:** Coaching to help you transition suc-cessfully into an organization, within an organization, or out of an organization.

Executive coaching often doesn't fit neatly into one of these catego-ries, but gaining clarity around your development needs is an essen-tial element in finding a good match with an executive coach.

Finding the right executive coach for you

There are various coaching federations that certify coaches in an attempt to bring some order to the profession, the most well known is the International Coach Federation (ICF), which has sixteen thou-sand members in more than ninety countries. Selecting an ICF or other accredited coach will at least guarantee you a certain level of experience and quality. However, the best way to find a good executive coach is to get a few referrals from your business network, including your HR department, which may already have contacts with some tried and tested coaches. Meet each referred coach for a preliminary meeting to find out about his or her training and experience and to establish the best match for your development needs. Once you have made your selection, you will agree on the objectives of the coaching, how you will work together to achieve those objectives, the duration of the contract, and the frequency of your meetings.

Many organizations are seeing the benefit of executive coaching and are increasingly willing to fund this type of development. If your organization is willing to support you in this way, it is a clear signal that you are highly valued—good executive coaching doesn't come cheap. In late 2005, the *Harvard Business Review* calculated that

American companies were spending more than $1 billion annually on coaching.

In 2008 the ICF commissioned independent research firms PricewaterhouseCoopers (PwC) and the Association Resource Centre, Inc., to gather reliable, in-depth data on the ever-growing number of people worldwide that have experienced professional coaching.[81] This research explored client perceptions about the industry, their motivations for engaging in coaching, how they went about selecting a coach, their assessment of the effectiveness of coaching, the return on investment and more. Survey respondents included 2,165 coaching clients from sixty-four countries. Some of the highlights include:

- 96.2 percent of coaching clients report they would repeat their coaching experience.

- 82.7 percent of coaching clients report they were "very satisfied" with their coaching experience.

- The top three motivations for obtaining coaching were: 1) Self-esteem/Self-confidence (40.9 percent); 2) Work/Life balance (35.6 percent); and Career Opportunities (26.8 percent).

- The duration for the average coaching relationship for survey participants was 12.8 months.

- 65 percent of coaching clients were female.

Executive coaching is a fantastic opportunity to benefit from targeted, personalized development that can accelerate and boost your career. Just ensure that you don't settle for anything less than an excellent coach who has the appropriate training and experience, who understands the specific challenges that women leaders face, and who can partner with you to make it one of the most challenging and developmental experiences of your career.

Chapter Eight

Personal Sustainability

> **UNWRITTEN RULE:**
> ### Senior leaders are available anytime and anywhere
> **This means:**
> - They are always available. Full-time work is the norm and part-time work is out of the question or career limiting.
>
> - They must be physically present in an office for ten or more hours per day, with little or no flexible working or working from home.
>
> - They travel extensively as part of their job.

Jane is a very talented and dedicated leader and is currently a high-potential candidate for a more senior leadership position in her organization. She likes the company she works for and aspires to lead one of their major divisions. She has credibility with her bosses, and her geographically dispersed team consider themselves lucky to have her as their leader. In many ways, she is a role model leader in her organization. Behind the scenes, however, Jane is finding it increasingly difficult to manage her energy in all parts of her life. As demands on her have increased, her capacity to respond effectively on all fronts has decreased. She is working longer and longer hours, surviving on too little sleep, missing meals, and resorting to fast food on the run. She uses caffeine to get her going in the morning and, in the evening, she relies on alcohol to help her relax. Of most concern to Jane is that she has become increasingly short tempered with her husband and children.

Like many corporate leaders, Jane is stuck inside a structure where it is difficult for her to step back and get the perspective she needs to see the real impact of the choices she is making. In fact, to Jane, it doesn't feel like she has choices. She lives in a world where 24/7 is common language describing a lifestyle where work never ends. Modern technology enables her to be in touch and responsive all of the time and her personal and work lives have become integrated rather than separate. Overwork in today's corporate environment has, for many, become an addiction that is admired and rewarded, unlike most other addictions.

In Japan the dire consequences of overwork have become so endemic that they now warrant a specific term, Karōshi, the literal translation of which is "death from overwork." The major medical causes of Karōshi deaths are heart attack and stroke due to stress. Japan is one of the few countries to track this statistically as a separate category. Some ten thousand deaths per year are attributed to Karōshi. If you think this has nothing to do with work environments in North America and Europe, think again. In her excellent book *Off-Ramps and On-Ramps. Keeping Talented Women On The Road To Success,* Sylvia Ann Hewlett describes what she calls "extreme jobs." A person is considered to have an extreme job if he or she is well paid, works sixty hours or more per week, and has at least five of the following extreme job characteristics:

- Unpredictable flow of work.

- Fast-paced work under tight deadlines.

- Inordinate scope of responsibility that amounts to more than one job.

- Work-related events outside regular work hours.

- Availability to clients 24/7.

- Responsibility for profit and loss.

- Responsibility for mentoring and recruiting.

- Large amount of travel.

- Large number of direct reports.

- Physical presence at workplace at least ten hours a day.

Hewlett says that 2005/2006 global surveys from the United States, Canada, Europe, the Middle East, and Africa reveal that 45 percent of senior workers have extreme jobs.

"Extreme jobs are spreading and are now all over the economy, in large manufacturing companies as well as in medicine and the law; in consulting, accounting, and the media as well as in financial services. They are prevalent on a global scale and are held by fifty-five-year-olds as well as thirty-five-year olds. Extreme jobs are not a young person's game or a short-term sprint anymore. Rather, they characterize the beginning, middle, and tail end of many careers."[82]

The *unwritten rule* of "availability anytime, anywhere" and the spread of "extreme jobs" for those in senior leadership positions aren't going away. This means that, as a woman who is either in or aspiring to higher-level positions within today's organizations, you need to develop the orientation and ability to manage your energy and sustain yourself. It's not that you can't succeed if you don't effectively manage your energy; it's just that you seriously compromise your performance, health, and general well-being by not doing so. The aim is to perform at your best for eight–twelve hours per day, be enthusiastic about getting to work in the morning, look forward to getting home in the evening, and stay healthy.

Manage your energy as well as your time

There are thousands of books and hundreds of workshops that can help you manage your time. Time management is essentially using a range of skills, tools, and techniques to accomplish specific goals, projects, and tasks. These are likely to include goal-setting, planning, delegation, organizing, scheduling, prioritizing, and monitoring. Through necessity, most professional women I know are pretty good at managing their time and proud of their ability to multitask and deliver what they set out to achieve. They have successful full-time careers and usually take a primary role in managing their families and their homes. They even occasionally find space for themselves, although this tends to be the first thing to go when time pressures increase. Managing time in a way that enables you to tick most of the boxes on your to-do list is valuable, but no guarantee that you produce the quality of energy needed to succeed to higher levels of organizational leadership, stay healthy, and have a fulfilling life outside of work.

In Section One of this book, we highlighted the phenomenon that women often need to outperform their male counterparts to be considered for senior leadership positions. To sustain such high performance, it is helpful to think about how we gain energy and where we invest it in order to operate at our best. The fact that there are only twenty-four hours in each day is something we cannot change, no matter how dynamic and enthusiastic we are about our work. Where we do have control is over the quality and quantity of the energy that we invest in the things that matter most to us, including our work.

Teaching your grandmother to suck eggs

For those of you who are not familiar with this expression, it is an old British proverb that warns about giving needless or unwanted advice to others who probably know more about the subject than you do. Presumably at one point in British history people were trying to give advice to grandmothers who had lost their teeth and had become experts in sucking eggs. (For those of you whose interest has been piqued, type this proverb into Google and you will get more information than you ever needed to know on the subject.) What, might you ask, does this have to do with managing your energy?

It would be easy and somewhat formulaic to now launch into giving you advice that you already know and have probably read or heard a hundred times before. Such as, to keep fit and healthy and perform at your best you should:

- ❑ Sleep seven–eight hours per night.

- ❑ Always eat breakfast.

- ❑ Eat a balanced, healthy diet.

- ❑ Eat little and often.

- ❑ Drink forty-eight ounces of water daily.

- ❑ Take regular breaks at work.

- ❑ Exercise daily, mixing cardiovascular and strength training.

- ❑ Minimize your caffeine, alcohol, and simple sugar consumption

There isn't one organizational leader I have coached who hasn't already discovered or received this good advice. Very occasionally, I even come across someone who is acting on it. Knowing what we need to do to manage our physical energy isn't usually the issue. Working out if we want to do what it takes and how to achieve it within the structure of today's intense organizational life seems to be the challenge.

A holistic approach

To make good choices in service of better performance and a healthier and more fulfilling lifestyle requires a holistic approach to personal sustainability. The term "personal sustainability" is commonly used to describe individual actions that contribute to saving the environment. In the context of women and leadership, however, I am using the term to describe a different concept. What we will be exploring in this chapter are actions you can take to sustain yourself in your many roles as leaders, mothers, life partners, and healthy human beings. Lack of focus and action to support yourself personally and professionally is shortsighted and often results in unnecessary stress, possible illness, and thwarted career progress. It is not good leadership practice to take a macho "I can do it all myself" approach and sets a bad example for people below you in the organizational hierarchy. Fortunately, there are pragmatic actions you can and should take to ensure your own well-being and support your aspirations to lead within today's organizations. Do not expect your organization to present you with a personal sustainability plan. You need to take responsibility for developing and sustaining yourself.

Personal sustainability isn't just about physical energy. It is essentially a dynamic system of four key elements:

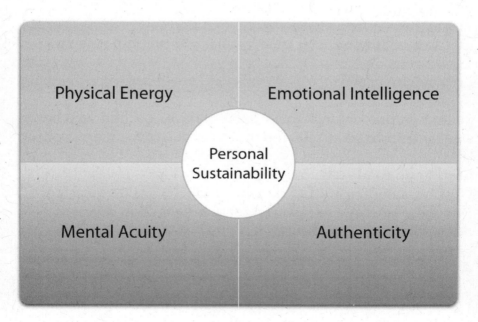

Like all integrated, dynamic systems, these four elements are inter-related; change in any one of these areas will have some impact on the others. The good news, therefore, is that positive action in any one of these areas is likely to have a positive impact on some or all of the other areas. The bad news is that the converse is equally true.

1. Physical energy

This is our fundamental source of fuel. Without sufficient sustainable physical energy we stand little chance of being emotionally connected, mentally focused, and authentically aligned. It's like the gas tank in your car; without sufficient fuel, you are unlikely to reach your destination in good shape. There are things you can do to increase the fuel in your tank to ensure that you perform at your best for eight–twelve hours a day, be enthusiastic about getting to work in the morning, look forward to getting home in the evening, and stay healthy. I'm sure you don't want to hear this again, but it's important, and so I am going to repeat it:

- ❑ Sleep seven–eight hours per night.

- ❑ Always eat breakfast.

- ❑ Eat a balanced, healthy diet.

- ❑ Eat little and often.

- ❑ Drink forty-eight ounces of water daily.

- ❑ Take regular breaks at work.

- ❑ Exercise daily, mixing cardiovascular and strength training.

- ❑ Minimize your caffeine, alcohol, and simple sugar consumption.

There is no getting away from the basic maintenance we need to do on our body to stay healthy. If this list represents a dramatic change in your lifestyle, do not despair. We will look later at how your orientation and your choices can support you in making some small changes that can have a big impact.

2. Emotional intelligence

Leaders with good emotional intelligence and positive emotional energy attract people who want to follow them. They exhibit self-confidence, effective interpersonal behavior, empathy, patience, openness, and trust. Great leaders demonstrate these qualities even in times of considerable stress.

Leaders with poor emotional intelligence and negative emotional energy are often described as "toxic." They lack self-control and lead through manipulation, fear, anger, and defensiveness. Not only do they create a negative working environment, but they do great self-harm. Persistent negative emotions often lead to poor health, ranging from headaches and back pain to heart disease and cancer.

Emotional and physical energy go hand-in-hand. It is impossible to be in good shape emotionally inside and outside of work, if your physical energy is seriously depleted. Positive emotion and behaviors not only support your own high performance and career progression, they also have a profound impact on the people that you manage and lead. Positive emotional intelligence helps to create and sustain good working relationships. The 2006 Gallup study, *"Feeling good matters in the workplace,"* concluded that a positive relationship with your boss has a significant impact on how happy and engaged you are at work (we probably didn't need a survey to tell us this, but it's nice to have it confirmed).[83] In terms of managing your emotional energy, therefore, it is not only important from the perspective of your own well-being and leadership capacity, it also has a profound impact on your organization and the people you lead. Organizing your life in a way that includes renewing your physical energy and developing good emotional intelligence should ideally be part of your leadership practice. Building on the positive influence behaviors in Chapter Five will not only enable you to influence more effectively, but also develop and manage your emotional energy (go to www.unwrittenrulesthebook.com for information on workshops for women leaders).

3. Mental acuity

Mental acuity is our ability to think strategically, solve problems, and be creative and innovative. Both physical and emotional energy feed into our mental capacity. It is interesting that people are usually promoted to positions of senior leadership based partly on their ability to think effectively at a strategic level. And yet leaders in today's organizations are rarely given or take time out to renew their mental energy and to think. Instead, they are constantly reacting and responding to the increasing demands that come their way.

In most large organizations the explicit and implicit message is that working continuously for long hours is the path to higher performance and career progression. Leaders are not generally encouraged or rewarded for taking regular breaks or interrupting their pattern of work to reflect and consider. Even though most of us know that this probably doesn't make sense, the somewhat "macho" nature of most organizational environments makes it difficult to buck the trend and step outside of what is generally acceptable. One of the great benefits of executive coaching is that leaders are legitimately able to interrupt their normal work activity to think, reflect, and sharpen their mental acuity.

4. Authenticity

This is about aligning our behavior with a deeply held set of values. Behaving in alignment with our values, or being true to ourselves, is always aspirational—I have never met anyone who unfailingly lives in accordance with his or her values all of the time, but we can certainly aspire to this. As an organizational leader, connecting with your values on a regular basis will support and enable you to feel centered and grounded, and to make good choices that enable you to sleep well at night.

To be meaningful, our values must influence our behavior. Leaders are judged on how they live their values, not what they espouse them to be. As a leader you are constantly under a spotlight that reveals whether or not you behave in alignment with your own and your company's values. The leadership challenge is to find a way to express and live by our values in the workplace. In Chapter Nine we will explore further the challenges and conflicts this presents to all leaders in today's organizations and, in particular, to women leaders.

A holistic approach to personal sustainability requires first that you are aware of the four dynamic elements: physical energy, emotional intelligence, mental acuity, and authenticity. Second, you must decide whether or not you believe that focusing on and managing these four dimensions will help make you be a better leader and enhance your career prospects. Third, you must believe it to be possible for you to make changes that will give you the physical energy, emotional intelligence, mental acuity, and authenticity to: perform at your best for eight–twelve hours per day, be enthusiastic about getting to work in the morning, look forward to getting home in the evening, and stay healthy.

Your choice

It is not my intention to persuade you that attending to your personal sustainability will support you in succeeding within the *unwritten rule* of "available anytime, anywhere," but I do suggest that the only way you can really find out is to give it a try. I believe that paying attention to personal sustainability will support any leader working within the extreme demands of today's organizations. I also see plenty of evidence that it is possible to succeed to higher positions of leadership by sacrificing your health and relationships. Personal sustainability is not a prerequisite for success, but I do think it is essential if you want to (here it comes again) perform at your best for eight–twelve hours per day, be enthusiastic about getting to work in the morning, look forward to getting home in the evening, and stay healthy.

This leaves the question of viability. Is it is possible to make changes in the way that you think about and manage your personal sustainability within the demands of the role you have right now? Given the intense pressure already on your organizational and personal life, does it become just one more burden, or is it a key that could unlock even higher levels of performance and a more enjoyable life outside of work?

Good reasons why you haven't got time for personal sustainability

There are, of course, many good reasons why we can't do the things necessary to manage our personal sustainability:

- There are not enough hours in the day to exercise/eat properly/take breaks, etc.

- I travel so much that it is impossible to get into any sort of routine that will support my health and energy management.

- I have tried exercising many times in the past, but never keep it up because I don't enjoy it.

- I only enjoy exercising outside and it's too cold/too hot/too dark/too wet.

- I can't organize my day because I don't have full control over my schedule and I'm constantly being pulled into mandatory meetings.

- I don't have time to take breaks during the day and, even if I did, it would not look good to my boss and colleagues.

- The CEO in my company manages through fear and emotional outbursts and so it's OK for me to do the same—it's clearly the way to get to the top around here.

- I am performing perfectly well at the moment, thank you very much, without giving personal sustainability any special attention.

- If I have any time at all I want to spend it with my family, not exercising or taking time for myself.

- Write any additional good reasons of your own here

- _____

Orientation

Robert Fritz,[84] who has written many books on the creative process, describes two very different orientations: a reactive/responsive orientation and a generative/creative orientation. If you have a reactive/responsive orientation, your circumstances are in control and are the driving force in your life. All of the statements above about not having the time, or the right circumstances to support you in attending to your personal sustainability are a reaction or a response to circumstances. Fritz writes:

> "We are taught that circumstances are the power in our lives, and that we should just learn how to deal with them. Questions about what matters to you are irrelevant if you only can respond to your circumstances in which you find yourself ... In our society, you are thought to have progressed if you move from reacting to responding. However, in each case the circumstances are still the dominant factor in your life."[85]

There is little chance of managing your personal sustainability in a way that unlocks higher levels of performance and supports a more enjoyable life outside of work if you stay in a reactive/responsive orientation. There will always be circumstances that give you reason to believe that you can't exercise, eat well, take breaks, and do whatever else it takes to renew yourself.

In this orientation you are likely to oscillate between implementing changes that support you in being healthy and managing your energy and emotions, then swinging back to neglecting yourself as the circumstances take over. In effect, you become a victim of your circumstances rather than the generative force in your own life. A victim mentality is not the orientation of an effective leader.

In a generative or creative orientation you, rather than the circumstances, are the dominant force. It's not that the circumstances disappear, but rather they become factors to be taken into consideration in the context of generating what you want. You cease to become a victim of your circumstances but you understand them as forces in play when creating what you want.

You probably already know, deep down, that the list of "good reasons" above are really a bunch of excuses; good excuses, but still excuses. If something is really important to you, you know that you can and probably will make it happen. If you are not currently managing your personal sustainability in a way that supports you performing at your best for eight–twelve hours per day, being enthusiastic about getting to work in the morning, looking forward to getting home in the evening, and staying healthy—and you think this is important— you are likely to be reacting to circumstances rather than being the generative force in your own life. A shift from a circumstantial to a generative orientation is essential; not only in managing your energy, but also in a more holistic sense of creating the life that you want. For a more in-depth exploration of these different orientations, I recommend *Your Life As Art* by Robert Fritz.[86]

Stories from the front line

If you aspire to, or are in, a senior leadership position in an organization today, you are inevitably operating within the context of the "available anytime, anywhere" *unwritten rule*. This rule—and the "extreme jobs" it breeds—shows no sign of changing. If you want to operate at your highest potential and give yourself the best chance of succeeding to and sustaining a senior leadership position, it makes sense to ensure that you are managing your personal sustainability, as well as your time. People who have realized this are moving away from being a victim of their circumstances and creating changes and habits in their lives that enable them to operate at a higher level, have a life outside of work, and stay healthy.

Small changes can often make a big difference. During a recent coaching session I suggested to my client, Gord Cooper, that we get out of the office and continue our coaching walking in the cold, bright sunshine. I did this because he was looking tired, run down, his energy was low, and I know that he renews himself by doing things outside. The thirty-minute walk that we took not only revitalized him for the rest of the coaching session, it also set in motion a change in behavior that is helping him to manage his energy during his very hectic days. He now makes it a regular habit to periodically disengage from the work he is doing during the day and go for a walk, either around his building to talk to others or to walk outside and clear his mind. He also plans to have meetings with a colleague walking outside so that they can both benefit from some fresh air and a change of scene. This small change in behavior has had a surprisingly significant impact on his energy during the day, so much so that he has also now decided to start jogging with a colleague after work. When we reflected on this at a later coaching session his quite profound observation was that "sometimes life just gets in the way of living better."

Theresa Firestone, general manager for Established Products at Pfizer, Canada, always seems to have lots of positive energy, looks younger than her years, has a very active personal life, and rarely seems stressed-out by her very demanding job. When I asked her how she manages her personal sustainability to achieve this she told me:

"I love my job and would not be excited by working nine to five. I am always very busy but I wouldn't be happy any other way. The position I have always taken with my bosses is that I will work hard and get the work done, but I need flexibility to manage my time. I make it clear to my manager that even if I have to leave early on some days the work will get done. I often block out time in my calendar and my assistant will then have to check with me if she wants to take it. If I don't do this, I could spend the entire day in meetings.

"I get into work early, usually around 7:00 a.m., so that I have the first hour of the day to get caught up and I try to leave before 6:00 p.m. It's still a long day but it's important for me to go home and have dinner with my family. Even though my kids have now left home, I still make sure I get away to have dinner with my husband. This gives me a certain grounding and enables me to take a break. I am also lucky enough to have a husband who gives me a reality check whenever I am working too many hours without a break. It's a good check and balance for me. I quite often work on weekends, but it's interesting that when I *don't* do this I have more energy and I am more productive on Monday.

"I don't have a formal exercise routine, but I do jog and cycle with my husband, and we walk a lot. We also organize events in the calendar, which ensures that I do things other than work. What I love to do that really enables me to take a break is to read—to me it's like eating chocolate cake."

In 2007, *Fast Company Magazine* ran an article citing examples of what people in high-stress jobs were doing to manage their lives and stay on top of things.[87] Maggie Wilderotter, Christina Maslach, Frank Sesno, and Carisa Bianchi are four examples from this article of different approaches to personal sustainability:

Maggie Wilderotter
President, Director, and CEO,
Wink Communications Inc.
Alameda, California

"I know that it's time to recharge my batteries whenever I look at my schedule and see that every single minute of the day is booked. People often say (especially to someone who runs a company), 'This is no time for a break!' But that's precisely when I tell my assistant, 'I need a half hour to go on a "lion hunt." When I go on a lion hunt, I'm totally off the charts. That means that my assistant holds all of my calls and rejiggers my schedule, canceling anything that isn't a priority. And then I begin my hunt: I prowl through the office, asking people what they're working on. That gives me a chance to connect with employees whom I don't usually talk to. Lion hunts are incredibly relaxing because—even if they last just thirty minutes—they take me away from a demanding schedule that requires me to push, push, push. And I always walk away from the experience having learned something: I have a renewed understanding of what we're doing at my company.

"I've never burned out on the job, simply because I don't let myself get to that point. You've got to be able to pace yourself and allow time for plenty of breaks. I have three golden rules: Weekends are for my family, not for my work; I take four weeks of vacation each year; and I try to maintain a healthy lifestyle—by sleeping enough, eating well, and exercising often.

"Time is a finite resource, and we all place infinite demands on it. I view time as an opportunity, as a chance to make choices about how I spend that resource—because it is our choice. And that's something that people often forget."

Christina Maslach, Professor of Psychology, University of California Berkeley, California

"I hear lots of people in organizations complain that their job never ends: 'I'm here until 8:00 p.m., 9:00 p.m., 10:00 p.m. I'm never home.' Whenever I ask them why they do it, they say that if they didn't, then coworkers would see them as not doing their fair share—and call them a wimp.

"But when you work long hours, you burn out. And often, there's no real reason for it. People assume that their workplace has a 'norm' when it really doesn't. So a companywide ignorance develops. Since people don't talk about how they're struggling, everyone thinks that everyone else is handling things fine. Companies with employee burnout have major communication work to do.

"But what about individuals? We can each do something to ensure that we get some relief. I build certain rituals into my weekly and monthly calendars. That's the only way to make sure that I do things that I enjoy and that energize me. You must learn to fence off certain parts of your life, to protect those chunks of time, and to decide for yourself how you're going to use them. Because if you don't, then someone else will.

"Ritualizing an activity by adding it to your calendar helps ensure that you do it. It's also important to notice what you say to yourself about how you're handling your time. People often say, 'I don't have the time,' when what they mean is that they've told themselves that they need to be available in case something else comes up. You have to make taking care of yourself a priority."

Frank Sesno
Senior Vice President and
Washington Bureau Chief, CNN
Washington, DC

"I know people who go for a walk at lunchtime, or who swim every day, or who meditate in the office. I'm not one of those people. You can't get away from the news; it's history in the making. And I've got a front-row seat. It gets crazy around here. Working in a newsroom is like working in an emergency room: You're likely to have a major disaster at any moment.

"Spending time with my kids (who are sixteen, twelve, and ten) helps me face another day of news. Lately, I've been reading the Harry Potter books with my daughter. I want to be the best dad possible—and to do the best job at work that I can. But there are times when you can't do both. You have to be able to recognize those times and make tough choices.

"In 1988, CNN asked me to be its primary political reporter on all news pertaining to Michael Dukakis and his presidential campaign. At the time, my older son was three, and my wife and I had just had our second child. I was already on the road a lot, and the Dukakis coverage would have taken me away from home even more. One night, I called my wife while she was tucking our three-year-old son into bed. She said to him, 'Let's say good night to Daddy, even though he's not here.' My son said, 'I hate Daddy. I don't want him to go away again forever.' Those were his exact words. That woke me up. When CNN asked, 'Can you go on the road with Dukakis?' I said, 'Sorry, I just can't do that.'"

**Carisa Bianchi, President and CEO, TBWA/
Chiat/Day
San Francisco, California**

"I worked on the Energizer Bunny campaign. And let me tell you, that little creature's very similar to advertising executives: we keep going and going. That's why I try to set an example in my office. I draw a clear line between my work life and my personal life, and I expect my coworkers to do the same. Otherwise, we'll all burn out.

"Everyone needs to leave work behind sometimes. I never work on airplanes—no computer, no phone, no nothing. For most businesspeople, airplanes are their favorite place to work. But people in my office know not to expect anything from me when I'm flying. It's a hard-and-fast rule: Once I'm on the plane, my time is my time. I read books and magazines, and I listen to music—things that I don't usually have time to do.

"You can always find reasons to work. There will always be one more thing to do. But when people don't take time out, they stop being productive. They stop being happy, and that affects the morale of everyone around them."

Moving to action

If you think that your ability to lead more effectively in your current role and your chances of succeeding to higher leadership positions will be supported by managing your personal sustainability more effectively; and if you value your relationships, your family, and a fulfilling life outside of work, it's time to think about and plan changes that suit you, your career and your lifestyle.

Any changes in work or lifestyle habits clearly need to be within the context of the "available anytime, anywhere" *unwritten rule* and the individual commitments required from leaders with extreme jobs. You may not be able to change many of the circumstances and pressures that you find yourself operating within, but it is possible to think differently and implement some small changes that can make a big difference.

Developing a generative/creative orientation

Developing a generative/creative orientation is about choosing to be the generative force in your own life, rather than being the victim of your circumstances. This is not about positive thinking. It's about identifying what you want to achieve, understanding the context in which you want to achieve it and then taking actions that will move you toward your desired end results.

Developing a generative orientation applied to personal sustainability requires that you first recognize where you may have been positioning yourself as a victim of your circumstances (perhaps revisit the list of reasons "why you haven't got time for this" above) and instead make some choices about end results that you want to achieve, even though those circumstances exist.

For example, at the time of writing this book I am a full-time consultant and executive coach; I run my own small business; I travel extensively to other countries to work; I am a wife and a mother; and my family and good friends are dispersed across different continents. Adding in a time-intensive commitment like writing a book to my already full life requires that I not only make choices about what I want, but that I also attend to my personal sustainability in a way that gives me the best chance of getting it. I don't want to generate my end result (the book) at the expense of my health or my relationships. I need the quality and quantity of energy necessary to continue my full lifestyle and create the things I want—in this case, a book.

My first step was to make a clear choice about what I wanted: to have written a book on women and leadership within twelve months of my start date. As part of my process toward this goal, I looked at the same four separate, but related, sources of personal sustainability (physical energy, emotional intelligence, mental acuity, and authenticity), then made informed choices about some investments I needed to make to ensure that I had the quantity and quality of energy needed to accomplish everything I wanted. I realized that I would benefit from changes in the physical sector, as I had already organized my life in such a way that I was already well invested in being emotionally connected, mentally engaged, and true to myself (the result of a lot of learning and change in my life over the preceding ten years).

Three very simple but key areas of change for me in generating more physical energy (which allowed me the mental acuity I needed to write this book), were:

1. Yoga. I introduced a regular and consistent yoga practice into my weekly schedule. This form of exercise revitalizes me

physically and mentally and I am able to continue it in my hotel rooms when I am traveling.

2. Breaks. I have learned to take regular breaks every one and a half to two hours, particularly when I am writing. These might be as simple as talking to my husband and son for twenty minutes, or taking a walk for half an hour to clear my head.

3. Dietary changes. I have made some small changes to my diet to include less caffeine, alcohol, and simple sugars.

These three actions do not represent a massive change in my lifestyle, but they are all simple changes that have contributed to my physical energy and mental acuity that have supported me in accomplishing this book.

Recovery is the key

If you are in a leadership position in an organization, it is probably not viable to manage your personal sustainability more effectively by reducing the challenges that you face on a daily basis. These challenges are part of your job as a leader and evidence shows that they are getting more, rather than less, extreme. The key to personal sustainability is not to reduce the challenge, but to identify what helps you to recover and renew your energy, stay mentally sharp and emotionally connected to others, and to integrate these activities into your daily schedule.

The concept of enhancing performance by alternating periods of activity with periods of recovery forms the basis of most high-performance sports training. The science of periodization dictates that energy expended must be recovered if athletes are to sustain maximum performance. Every top athlete knows that the amount of energy renewal needs to be commensurate with the degree of energy expended.

As a woman leading in today's organizations, it might be helpful to think of yourself as a corporate athlete. To perform at your best eight–twelve hours per day and to sustain this over the years it takes to succeed to senior leadership positions, it helps to build in renewal activities as part of your regular schedule.

Renewal is very personal and needs to fit your preferences. For Theresa Firestone, reading helps her to take a break from her intense organizational life and is so pleasurable, it's like "eating chocolate cake." One of my Canadian coaching clients loves the outdoors so much that he finds shoveling snow renews his physical and mental energy. Other women I have come across have built in recovery time by:

- Taking a twenty-minute catnap during the afternoon.

- Taking a thirty-minute break at a local coffee shop.

- Taking lunch on a park bench or in a local gallery two or three times per week.

- Taking lunch at their desks listening to music on their headphones.

- Regularly having dinner with their family, bathing the kids, and putting them to bed.

- Getting up early every day and walking for forty-five minutes before their family gets up.

- Winding down every night by taking a bath, drinking herbal tea, and reading light fiction.

- Getting all of their thoughts out of their heads by writing in a journal each night before they go to bed.

- Taking dance classes after work.

- Gardening on the weekend.

- Creating a regular dinner date, just for two, with their husband.

- Taking local adult education classes that have nothing to do with their jobs.

- Engaging in ten minutes of breathing exercises at their desks each day.

- Doing twenty minutes of yoga in their offices each afternoon.

- Going to church every Sunday.

- Painting.

- Getting a professional massage every Friday.

- Taking long weekends away with their spouses four times per year.

- Watching their kids play soccer and hockey.

- Eating breakfast with someone interesting once per week.

- Enjoying drinks with girlfriends.

- Taking lunch away from their desks every day.

Right now, it might be helpful to think about and write down what you like to do that helps you to disengage from your intense work routine and renew your energy. What helps you to feel physically energized emotionally connected, mentally engaged, and authentically true?

Ritualizing and scheduling the activity

If I don't schedule my yoga practice into my weekly schedule, it doesn't happen. Making it part of my week and scheduling my work around it works most of the time. (I'm not perfect.) Whatever you choose to do that helps you to sustain yourself, make it a regular and ritualized part of your week. This means building it into your daily and weekly schedule and treating it as an important part of your day. Building in recovery activities that renew your physical, emotional, mental, and spiritual energy need to become habits that you hardly have to think about, it's just how you operate. It also helps to reframe what you are doing. If in the past you have seen it as taking a break or "veging out," it might help to see it as investment and renewal time.

A simple plan

Change does not have to be dramatic. In fact, it is often difficult to sustain dramatic changes in our lifestyle. Try making small changes and if they work you are likely to be encouraged to make some more. For example, taking a walk around the building or outside in the fresh air was not a dramatic change for Gord Cooper, but he has been surprised at the positive impact on his physical and mental energy.

Step 1: Build your physical energy capacity

Unless you are already investing in renewing your physical energy on a regular basis, it's a good idea to start by identifying what helps you feel more physically energized. Without physical energy it is very difficult to be emotionally connected, mentally focused, and authentically engaged.

- Find one simple way that you can increase your physical exercise (e.g., take a twenty-minute walk sometime during the day or do some kind of exercise that you enjoy).

- Find one way that you can improve your eating habits (e.g., replace a sugary afternoon snack with some nuts or fruit; it can make a big difference if it becomes a habit. If you are unsure which foods are healthier than others go to www. nuval.com).

- Look at how much sleep you are getting on a regular basis. I know people who have trained themselves to survive on four or five hours of sleep per night so that they can have more work time. This is generally considered to be unhealthy and possibly even life shortening. Organize your life to consistently get seven–eight hours of sleep per night.

Step 2: Regularly disengage for short periods

Develop the habit of disengaging from your work for at least twenty minutes during the day to take some kind of recovery and renewal break (e.g., take a walk, go outside the building, chat to your colleagues, whatever works for you).

Step 3: Schedule activities you find pleasurable

Look at your schedule and block out time for some activities that you find pleasurable (e.g., spending time with your partner, getting a massage, taking a dance class; again, whatever works for you). Treat these blocks of time in the same way that you treat important meetings.

If you decide to move from being the victim of your circumstances to being the generative force in your own life the three simple steps above will be achievable and will help you sustain yourself more effectively in service of performing at your best for eight–twelve hours per day, being enthusiastic about getting to work in the morning, looking forward to getting home in the evening, and staying healthy. If you are successful in making small changes such as these, you are likely to be encouraged to continue making other changes that support your health, energy, and leadership practice. For further reading to support you in your quest for personal sustainability I recommend

The Power of Full Engagement by Jim Loehr and Tony Schwartz and *Younger Next Year for Women* by Chris Crowley and Henry Lodge.

Being more physically energized will certainly improve your mental acuity and support your capacity to be emotionally connected to others. Aligning your deeply held values with your leadership behavior within the constraints of your organizational culture and everyday work pressures is a more complex area that we will explore in Chapter Nine.

Chapter Nine

Authenticity: Can Women Leaders Be True To Themselves?

The question of authenticity and whether or not women leaders can be true to themselves permeates all of the *unwritten rules*. Authenticity in this context refers to our capacity to align our behavior with our core values. Can women leaders really be authentic within the structure of the *unwritten rules*, or must they conform to traditional male leadership values and behaviors in order to make it to the top?

The importance of authenticity features strongly in most good leadership development research and literature. It is generally believed that to become a credible leader requires that you understand fully the values, beliefs and assumptions that motivate you. Kouzes and Posner's First Law of Leadership states, "If you don't believe in the messenger, you won't believe the message," with the corollary, "You can't believe in the messenger if you don't know what the messenger believes."[88] In his book *Authentic Leadership*,[89] Bill George says, "After years of studying leaders and their traits, I believe that leadership begins and ends with authenticity. It's being yourself; being the person you were created to be." Robert Goffee, professor of organizational behavior at London Business School, believes that "Authentic leadership has become, the most prized organisational and individual asset."[90]

The Unwritten Rules of Senior Leadership in Today's Organizations

1. Senior leaders are available anytime and anywhere

This means:
- They are always available. Full-time work is the norm and part-time work is out of the question or career limiting.

- They must be physically present in an office for ten or more hours per day, with little or no flexible working or working from home.

- They must have total geographical mobility. It is career suicide to turn down a promotion because it is undesirable or inconvenient to move.

- They travel extensively as part of their job.

2. Senior leaders have a linear career path

This means:
- They have a continuous employment history with no career breaks.

- They typically make their career breakthrough in their 30's, with rare second chances if they miss the boat.

3. Senior leaders are competitive

This means:
- They are tough, strong and assertive.

- They are typically motivated by money and position.

- They value career and family, but when these values are in conflict, career takes precedence.

4. Senior leaders promote themselves

This means:
- They build relationships with people who can support their career progression.

- They speak confidently about their accomplishments.

- They know what they want and influence others to get it.

In a 2000 *Harvard Business Review* article, "*Why Should Anyone Be Led by You,*"[91] Robert Goffee and Gareth Jones actually raise the question: "Can Female Leaders Be True to Themselves?" They observe that gender stereotyping makes authentic behavior very difficult for women leaders and they say that women tend to respond to it in three ways: first, they might try to behave like men; second, they may try to collectively resist being forced into certain behaviors by launching campaigns to promote the rights and opportunities at work for women; and third, they may try to turn stereotyping to their personal advantage by, for example, being the "nurturer" at work, but doing this "with such wit and skill that they are able to benefit from it." All of these strategies, they believe, "reduce a woman's chances of being seen as a potential leader" and not only reinforces harmful stereotypes but "continues to limit opportunities for other women to communicate their genuine personal differences."

In my work in organizations, I see women in leadership positions doing what it takes to get to the top within the culture of their specific organization. For example, I have encountered women who conform to organizational leadership norms by being pushy and aggressive, which often results in promotion to senior positions but, of course, not being liked by many colleagues and direct reports. I have also seen women make choices that keep them on the senior leadership track, such as hiding a pregnancy until a promotion was secured, leaving a six-month-old child to work three thousand miles away for five days of the week, and sleeping only four hours per night, so that more time can be spent with family and keep up with the work. Not all women have to go to these extremes, but those who want to succeed to senior leadership positions in today's organizations are willing to make pragmatic choices that keep them in the line of succession by doing whatever it takes.

The question of being true to yourself within any organizational culture is one to be wrestled with by all leaders, male and female. For women, the *unwritten rules* create a structure within which they will most likely need to either not have children or leave the primary care of their family to others; exhibit tough, strong and assertive behaviors in addition to being nurturing and collaborative; speak about their accomplishments and promote themselves; and build relationship networks with people who can support their career. For many women (and some men) conforming to these *unwritten rules* creates a conflict in values and results in classic dilemmas:

Values	Dilemmas
I value my career and I value my family	I want children and I need to stay on track to be a senior leader
I value my career and I value my family	I want to be with my family and I need to be physically present at work for long hours
I value my career and I value my family	I want stability for my family and I need to be geographically mobile to take advantage of career opportunities
I value good relationships and being liked	I need to be tough, strong and assertive and I need to be warm, caring and collaborative
I value being judged by my results	I want my work to speak for itself and I need to promote myself
I value being rewarded on merit rather than who I know	I want my work to speak for itself and I need to network and influence people to get ahead
I value being true to myself and I value being a senior leader	I want to behave in alignment with my values and I need to conform to the unwritten rules

What is distressing or painful about a dilemma is having to make a choice we don't want to make, particularly when that choice involves a values conflict. Behaving in alignment with our values is easy when they are not competing against each other. For example, if I am a woman who does not want to have children and I want to devote myself to my career, my choice to stay on the track to senior leadership is more straightforward. If, however, I value having children and having a career, there is likely to be a conflict between staying on track and stepping off for a while to start a family. Women therefore have to make difficult choices that sometimes feel like compromising their values in order to become senior leaders. This is also true for some men, but it is often more so for women because of the conflicts inherent in the *unwritten rules.*

When we compromise ourselves by behaving in ways that do not align with our deeply held core values there is usually a price to pay. Existentialist theory tells us that if we are not living authentically in our lives, we lose meaning and can fall into chronic anxiety, boredom, and despair. I know that in my past life, when I lived out of alignment with some of my values, over time I became depressed and physically unwell.

Values conflicts certainly account for some of the angst I encounter when coaching women leaders in today's organizations. I often find women troubled by conflicts such as valuing career and family and feeling that one (usually family) is being compromised; or valuing health and career and finding that one (usually health) gets less attention; or valuing being rewarded on merit, but finding others (usually men) are being promoted because of who they know as well as how they have performed. This seems like an impossible situation. How can women achieve positions of senior leadership within the structure of the *unwritten rules* and at the same time live in alignment with their values and be true to themselves? There is no easy answer; but from experience, I do know that if you understand your hierarchy of values in any given situation, make clear primary and secondary choices, and "be yourself with skill," it will help you to be constructive in your approach to situations where your values are in conflict and also enable you be true to yourself.

Understanding your hierarchy of values in any given situation

Our core values tend to stay pretty consistent for all of our lives. They are part of who we are, what we believe in, the assumptions we make, and they inform our actions. In any given situation we may find that we have more than one of our values in play and that we have to make a choice about how to behave. For example, my good friend models the dress she has bought for a function we are attending that evening and asks me if I like it. I don't particularly like the dress and I am confronted with a choice between two of my values: kindness and honesty. If I am true to my value of kindness, I will tell her that I like the dress because there is no time to change it and I don't want to risk spoiling her evening. Or I can be true to my value of honesty and tell her I don't like the dress. What do I do?

I have to decide my hierarchy of values in this specific situation. I need to make a choice in that moment about whether honesty is more important to me than kindness, or kindness is more important to me than honesty. It's not that I am changing my values; both are still important. But in any situation where my values are in conflict, I need to decide which value takes precedence in that particular moment. My values stay the same, but the hierarchy—or what is most important—will change in different situations and at different times of my life. Many women experience the same shift in priorities in regard to family. They may have valued their careers more highly in their twenties and early thirties, but then valued family more in their mid-to-late thirties and forties. They always valued career and family, but the importance changed at different life stages. We are confronted with situations such as these all of the time and it helps to be conscious of how our values may be in conflict and the fact that we always have a choice.

Situation	Values Conflict	Potential Choices
To progress my career I need to take an oversees appointment, but my family refuses to move	I value being with my family and I value career progression	At this time in my life and my career, what is more important to me, more time with my family, or progressing my career?
To improve my prospects for promotion I need to build relationships with the right people in my organization, but I would rather spend the time just doing a good job	I value progressing my career and I value doing my best in my current role	Is it more important in this organization and at this point in my career to devote all of my time to my current role, or to take some of my time to build important relationships?
I want to exercise so that I am fit and healthy, but my job and my family take all of my time	I value my health and I value my job and my family	Will I put my job and my family before my health and fitness, or is my health important enough to take some time to exercise regularly?
I am naturally a collaborative and inclusive leader, but to get ahead in my organization I need to be more competitive and assertive	I value being collaborative and inclusive and I value becoming a senior leader in this company	Do I learn to become more competitive and assertive, or do I try to find a different environment in which to express my leadership potential?
I prefer to be understated and let my work speak for itself, but the people who get ahead around here seem to be good at promoting themselves	I value modesty and I value getting promoted	Do I learn how to promote myself, or do I remain modest and hope for the best?

Aspiring to become a leader in today's organizations within the structure of the *unwritten rules* creates a certain inevitability that you will be confronted with choices such as these quite frequently. The important point is to recognize that it is always a choice and that you can make the choice based on your hierarchy of values in any given situation. The alternative is to slip into a victim orientation that looks something like this:

"I can't progress my career and be a good mother." (poor me)

"I can't look after my health because my family and my job take up all my time." (poor me)

"I can't do a good job and take the time to build a professional relationship network." (poor me)

"I can't be myself and be a leader around here." (poor me)

By positioning yourself as a victim of your circumstances you take away your own personal power and you certainly do not demonstrate good leadership. There is always a choice, even though it may be a difficult one, and understanding that you can make that choice based on your hierarchy of values in any given situation enables you to take control of the decisions you are making and not be the victim of your circumstances.

Primary and secondary choices

In his seminal work, *The Path of Least Resistance*, Robert Fritz describes primary choices as "choices about major results" and secondary choices as "choices that help you take a step toward your primary result."[92] The nature of secondary choices is that they are often things we may not particularly like to do, but they are essential if we are to achieve our primary result. For example, if my primary choice is to lose ten pounds of excess weight, my secondary choices are likely to involve eating less and exercising more, neither of which I particularly want to do, but both are essential secondary choices if I want to achieve my primary result. If I want to finish writing this book within my deadline I need to make the secondary choice of sitting alone with my computer for many hours, rather than doing countless other things that I might find more enjoyable. In the same way, if my primary choice is to become a senior leader in today's organizations where the *unwritten rules* prevail, some of the secondary choices I might need to make are to be available anytime and anywhere; to avoid any lengthy career breaks; to be tough, strong, and assertive and to build relationship networks and promote myself. If I can't make these secondary choices because they do not align with my values or how I want to live my life, I might be better off making a different primary choice.

However, if you have made the choice to lead in today's organizations, it is essential to make secondary choices that will support you in achieving your primary result. You may not always like these secondary choices, such as working long hours away from your family, or sometimes being direct and assertive, but understanding that they are secondary choices in support of your primary result is likely to help you when the going gets tough. When you are feeling confronted because your choices are mutually exclusive—like eating chocolate cake or losing weight; spending more time with your children or being at work—it can be tempting to play the victim or manipulate yourself into making decisions based on guilt or fear of punishment. If I decide to forgo the chocolate cake because I will feel guilty if I eat it, or if I stay at work for longer hours because I fear that I will be negatively judged in some way if I leave before others, I am likely to feel resentful about what I am doing. I am also likely to feel like the victim of my circumstances rather than a woman who is making conscious choices in line with what she wants to achieve.

If you want to be a senior leader in today's organizations be aware that you will need to make secondary choices that you may not like, many of which will be as a consequence of the *unwritten rules* that are a reality of the current state of play for women. If these choices seriously conflict with your core values and how you want to create your life, you might find Section Three of this book inspirational and enlightening. But if you are able to make clear choices based on your hierarchy of values and what is most important to you in any given situation, it will support you in maintaining your authenticity as a leader and being true to yourself.

The key message here is to consciously make clear choices, rather than be a victim of your circumstances. If you want to become a senior leader in your organization, make it a primary choice. Conduct due diligence on your organization and understand the secondary choices you will need to make to support the primary result that you want. You will likely need to revisit your primary choice often to give meaning and context to the secondary choices you make on a daily basis. In other words, remind yourself why you are sometimes doing things you may not particularly like doing (because it is in support of your primary choice). And remember, it's your choice, no one is making you do this and you can always choose something different.

Being yourself with skill

I wish I had invented the phrase "being yourself with skill" because it very succinctly describes how you can operate as a leader within today's complex organizations and be authentic and true to yourself. I came across the phrase in an interview with Rob Goffee, professor of organizational behavior at London Business School, and Gareth Jones, visiting professor at Insead. When asked the question of what do leaders need to know and do, Jones replied, "Be yourself—more—with skill."[93] What he meant by this was that leaders need to be themselves because "followers want to be led by a person—not a role holder or a position-filler or a bureaucrat" and at the same time they need to know "when and where to conform." He went on to say: "To be effective, the leader needs to ensure his or her behaviors mesh sufficiently with the organisational culture to create traction."

I am not a believer in women leaders adopting the values and behaviors of male leaders if it compromises their own values and authenticity, although I do understand why many women take this route. Undoubtedly, in some organizations, they would not have made it to the top without doing so. The *unwritten rules* encourage women to be conformists and role players. Conform to these rules and play the traditional leadership role if you want to make it up the hierarchical ladder. It's hard to be authentic and true to yourself if you are frequently conforming and role-playing.

In my organizational experience I see leaders flourish when they are able to be themselves in ways that conform enough to be accepted and at the same time add value by bringing their own unique differences and contributions. As a woman this means understanding the organizational culture, including the *unwritten rules*, and using the full range of behaviors described in Chapter Five to be yourself with skill. Being yourself with skill requires that you read each situation and respond in a way that gets the job done and also builds or at least maintains your credibility and relationships with your colleagues and those you lead. It also means that you make sound judgments about when to challenge and when to conform. Increasing your self-awareness and your ability to flex between the eight influencing behaviors in Chapter Five will go a long way to helping you to blend authenticity, adaptation, individuality, and conformity.

Leadership is situational, which means that to be effective you need to adapt and change your behavior in different situations. Being yourself with skill is a way to lead authentically by reading each situation and responding in a way that conforms enough to be accepted and credible, but also allows you to bring your unique attributes and skills to achieve the results that you want. It means that you don't have to compromise your values, but you do have to be able to judge when to confront and challenge, and when to conform. Taking every challenge head-on is just as inadvisable as always maintaining the status quo.

If you want to progress your career in your organization, or bring about sustainable change, or break some of the *unwritten rules* it is essential to do this from a position of established acceptance and credibility. I have seen many women who are senior leaders break some of the *unwritten rules*, but first they became accepted as leaders who knew when to conform and when to challenge. One very successful woman told me the story of how she thought she had ruined her career by refusing an overseas posting because she chose to put her family first. In fact, she had already gained such credibility and respect in the organization as an outstanding leader that she got away with it and is still on track to potentially be one of the most senior leaders in her organization. I know other women leaders who break the "available anytime, anywhere" rule by creating a flexible work schedule to achieve a more balanced life, but to be in a position to do this they first had to prove themselves within the specific context of their organizations.

It can be difficult, but it is possible for you to lead and be authentic in today's organizations. It requires a heightened self-awareness of your own values and how they align or misalign with those of your organization; an understanding of your company culture, including the *unwritten rules* that are not explicit, but nevertheless determine a lot of organizational behavior; the ability to make good choices and judgments about when to challenge and when to conform enough to gain acceptance; and excellent influencing skills to maintain and build credibility as well as staying true to your own values. You are likely to find that you have a natural ability in some of these areas and not in others. In those where you don't, I strongly recommend that they become a focus of your professional development through coaching, mentoring, and targeted leadership development programs.

As I write this chapter in April 2009, the world has been plunged into an alarming economic crisis that is partly the result of poor judgment and dubious values on the part of some corporate leaders. Understandably there is a lot of cynicism about the way in which our corporations are structured and led. Many believe that the time is right for a different type and style of leadership. Some hope that this might create fertile ground in which women leaders can grow and become more accepted, respected, and appreciated. Women who want to lead and who are able make good choices in alignment with their values and who are able to be themselves with skill will be ideally positioned to step forward and fill the perceived void of corporate leaders who are able to maintain their authenticity, even under extreme pressure.

Section Three
Corporate Refugees

INTRODUCTION

Section One of this book answered the question of why there aren't more women in positions of senior leadership and introduced the concept of the *unwritten rules* and the particular challenges faced by women in today's organizations. Based on this information, Section Two provided essential professional development for women who aspire to higher levels of leadership within the context of these specific challenges and rules.

This final section, Corporate Refuges, provides something quite different. It speaks to those women who sometimes wonder if continuing to strive within the context of large corporations provides the most supportive environment and the best career route to suit their needs and aspirations.

For this part of the book I was privileged to interview interesting, dynamic women who live and work in different cultures and countries—in the United Kingdom, the United Arab Emirates, Africa, Holland, Ireland, Switzerland, Singapore, Columbia, Canada, and the United States. All of these women were once managers, directors, vice presidents, executive vice presidents, or general managers in traditional organizations who chose to change course and set off on different adventures. Their stories are important and relevant because they show us that there is always a choice about how we live our lives, pursue our careers, and realize our dreams and ambitions.

If traditional organizations provide the challenge and opportunity that you love, then striving within this context is absolutely the right thing for you. But if you find you increasingly question your current career path or you find yourself daydreaming about a different life, this final chapter is for you.

Chapter Ten

Corporate Refugees

Wanderer, your footsteps are
the road, and nothing more;
wanderer, there is no road,
the road is made by walking.
Antonio Machado

The women interviewed for this chapter are diverse in their backgrounds, their professions, their ages, and their circumstances. The common thread that unites them all is that they confronted their dissatisfaction and created positive change in their lives. Many didn't know exactly where they were heading when they resigned their corporate jobs and they all, in their own ways, continue to create their roads by walking them. In this chapter, you will not only hear their stories, their challenges, and their successes, but also their hard-earned lessons and seasoned advice.

Over half of the interviewees were women who had left management or leadership positions in large organizations to start their own businesses. Globally, more and more women are choosing the challenge of becoming self-employed. According to the Center for Women's Business Research, women-owned firms account for 40 percent of all U.S. privately held firms.[94] Statistics Canada's Labour Survey reports there were 877,000 self-employed women in Canada in 2006, accounting for about one-third of all self-employed persons (a growth of 18 percent since 1996).[95] Female entrepreneurship is also increasing in the U.K. where there are now more than one million self-employed women—a 17 percent rise since 2000.[96] In 2008 the U.K. Women's Enterprise Task Force surveyed more than one thousand women entrepreneurs, revealing some interesting statistics:

- 70 percent of those polled started their business because they wanted more flexible working conditions.

- 75 percent of respondents said work/life balance is better when you're running your own business.

- 86 percent said they would set up a business again.

- 78 percent gained greater independence once they became an entrepreneur.

- 66 percent have enjoyed increased confidence[97].

What follows are some of the stories behind such statistics.

Names

Sue Van Der Hout and **Susan Mey**

Previous lives

Sue was a lawyer with the Canadian Department of Justice, then a partner in a private law practice.

Susan was president of Kodak, Canada, then worldwide director of Integration with Kodak.

New lives

Sue is the founder and owner of the online magazine, Girlphyte (www.girlphyte.com), and an entrepreneur developing an interactive profiling program, Blooming Betty, that engages users about values, goals, and successes. She is also a part-time teacher at the Seymour Schulich School of Business, Toronto, Canada.

Susan is the founder and owner of the online, green lifestyle store, Green Cricket (www.greencricket.ca).

Motivation for change

Sue:

"I was approaching fifty and I felt that I just didn't want to limit myself anymore. I wanted to see if there were other things that I could do."

Susan:

"I think it was the culture that I experienced in large organizations throughout my career that ultimately led me to the realization that it did not fit well with the kind of culture that I find motivating and rewarding ... large organizations are very structured and bureaucratic, which can make it difficult for teams to operate effectively ... I'm very much a team-based leader. I like to try to build consensus, have diversity of thought, and get opinions from multiple different sources when I make a decision ... I think that because of the structure and bureaucracy of large organizations, it becomes extremely difficult to operate in that way ... I think it hampers the success of the organization and also becomes de-motivating for individuals ... One of the great things about starting your own business is that you can create the type of environment that you want."

How they did it

Sue:

"I did a lot of things after I left the law practice ... I spent more time with my family, took my mom on a cruise, took a writing course, renovated a property ... I enjoyed meeting people and became an incredible networker ... I then trained in family communications in Boston at the

Family Firm Institute and brought the first chapter of this institute to Canada and was the founding president for a while ... at this time I realized that my passion was helping women to realize success ... I really wanted to give something back to women and so I started a women's Web site called girlphyte.com ... I've now taken the knowledge that I gathered from Girlphyte and I'm working with a small team on a software program that will help women redefine success."

Susan:

"It was a difficult decision to leave Kodak and I thought about it for a long time ... I convinced myself that I would much rather have the stress of building something for myself and making it the way I wanted it to be than to just put up with things that I felt were a waste of time and energy ... after I left I took a break because I didn't know what I wanted to do next ... I took lots of holidays ... then I realized that I am young, I have lots of energy, and I really wasn't doing anybody any good, including myself, by sitting around ... I had an idea for a business that I'd had for some time and so I built a business plan to start this company ... I wanted to start an organization that I felt would be delivering something meaningful in the market ... that had the best technology ... the best people engaged in a very creative way ... so I chose an Internet-based business in the environmental field that brings a lot of young people, creativity, energy, and passion around the environmental movement with the best technology to support it ... I sold a minority stake in the business to investors to raise capital and Green Cricket was incorporated on Valentine's Day, 2008, and we launched the Web site in December 2008."

Challenges

Sue:

"My previous training as a lawyer made me fearful or unwilling to even visualize the possibility of failure ... and so one of the first things for me in coming to grips with the change was to recognize that I was already a success (and so the risk was acceptable) ... The insecurity that I'm never good enough no matter what I did was a real albatross ... it's much more manageable now because I've become more accepting of myself and I have very affirming people around me."

Susan:

"I think the biggest challenge is to stay focused and slowly build up each pillar of the business ... it's just a lot of hard work and dedication and knowing what the key success strategies are ... one of the main reasons small businesses fail is lack of capital ... having access to capital is extremely important, but there is never enough money, you always need more ... it's an ongoing struggle to make sure that you have the right financing."

Advantages

Sue:

"I always enjoyed intellectual challenge and I have that in spades because there are a million pieces to entrepreneurship and you can never control them all ... there's always something to do, to learn, to do something better, which I love ... the other thing is that I was always alone in litigation work. I sat at a desk usually for ten hours a day and there was very little need to spend a lot of time with clients ... it was very lonely, and so now I'm working with a team and I really love that. The other piece is I was always creative within the narrow scope of tax litigation, but what I'm finding now is an ability to add value and be creative in ways that I didn't expect."

Susan:

"The mainstream acceptance of the green proposition has been very encouraging ... most of the public, green or not, have been looking for a convenient and affordable way to live a healthier lifestyle ... that's why I set up the company and so that's been very rewarding ... I have more control over the company culture ... I hire people based on their specialty, but I don't limit them once they come into the organization ... our people get motivated because they are not in a box ... for example, my assistant has a master's degree in environmental science and when I interviewed her I couldn't believe she wanted the position of administrative assistant ... I told her that she should go off and work in a research organization and earn a lot more money ... but she said she wanted to work in this organization because she could run and grow and do things outside of her job and, if she was really good at it in two years from now, she could be an operations manager ... Whereas at somewhere like a Fortune 500 company it would take her years and years to reach this position ... people can be what they want to be here ... they have a huge spectrum of opportunity in front of them and I don't limit what they can achieve in this organization."

Advice

Sue:

"One of the greatest fears to overcome is the fear that if you leave your job you will never get that opportunity back. The key thing that I discovered is that there are a million opportunities. There may be a painful transition because change and transition are painful for most people; but there are a million companies and a million opportunities and so there is no need to be afraid."

Susan:

"Before deciding what you want to do next, take a break to clear your head and give your body what it needs ... Just take some time for yourself ... doing other things allows you to be more creative ... you really have to take a break to refresh your thoughts and get yourself back in the right frame of mind."

Names

Barbara Laskin and **Susan Macaulay**

Previous lives

Barbara was an Emmy-award-winning TV anchor and political reporter.

Susan was a director of public relations in a corporate communications consultancy.

New lives

Barbara is the founder and president of Laskin Media, a New York-based communication-training company (www.laskinmedia.com).

Susan is the founder and managing director of Strike Communications, a Dubai-based communication-training company (www.strike.ae); she is also the founder of the online magazine www.amazingwomenrock.com.

Motivation for change

Barbara:

"My job as a TV anchor and political reporter was invigorating and dynamic.... I interviewed presidents and I was very high profile in both Canada and New York ... but I'd been at it for twenty years and it was becoming increasingly stressful ... probably more importantly I was on my second marriage and wanted to start a family ... after concentrating on my career for so long I wanted to concentrate on my personal life."

Susan:

"After moving to the United Arab Emirates for my husband's work, I spent the first year trying to find a job ... I picked up a few small jobs here and there but I realized that I wasn't going to find work in my chosen profession as a public relations specialist ... I also learned that I don't do well in a corporate environment. I'm not a good order taker; I'm much better at giving people instructions and telling them what to do."

How they did it

Barbara:

"I thought I could make a good living and be successful if I used what I already knew and was good at ... I went back to school and took some night courses in communication at NYU and I started to read up on my competitors ... then I started to develop my own program ... and once I started to get involved in the next stage of my life, when I had a goal, it became easier ... my name recognition was helpful at the beginning, but as anyone will tell you, you are only as good as your last performance ... it was hard work because I'd never had to go out and get a client before ... previously my assignments had been given to me ... but this was entirely new, I'd never been an entrepreneur before."

Susan:

"I got involved in doing public speaking, coaching and training kind of by accident. A friend of mine invited me to do a workshop on public relations and through that one experience I discovered that I really enjoyed doing workshops and training ... I did one workshop, and then one grew to two, and two grew to five and it went from there ... this is one of the great things about the United Arab Emirates and being in a developing economy ... there are so many opportunities to do things that you might not otherwise have thought of doing or attempted in a more established business environment ... I love living in Dubai and my business is now established here."

Challenges

Barbara:

"At the beginning the biggest challenge was branding myself at something new ... and it took several years to really formulate who the company was, what it could do, and how it could benefit clients ... once I got that going the next thing was making certain that my small staff were the best they could be and that I scheduled myself appropriately to firstly make money, and secondly make certain that I was where I wanted to be for my family ... this was all a big juggling act that evolved and is no longer an issue today."

Susan:

"Fluctuating income has been a challenge ... I see myself as extremely risk averse ... starting my business in 1998, my revenues increased steadily ... despite the fact that I had periods where I had no business ... so I worry less now about fluctuating income because I have faith that eventually something will come in ... I've been doing this for ten years and I've developed a certain level of faith that things are going to work out."

Advantages

Barbara:

"The biggest plus is controlling my own schedule, controlling my hours, determining when I want to work ... for me that's the greatest dividend of working for yourself ... I love the freedom ... I love the ability to do my own thing--by myself, for myself."

Susan:

"Freedom is very important to me and I don't have a daily schedule ... I arrange my own days ... I wake up in the morning and unless I have a workshop or some coaching, my day kind of evolves as it will ... I was miserable when I was in a box ... now I am much happier."

Advice

Barbara:

"For those out there who have a yearning to be their own boss, who have a yearning to do it themselves for whatever reason ... the only advice I have, and it's not unique but it is heartfelt, is DO IT ... if this is something that's gnawing at you and is really in your heart, chances are you are going to be successful ... if you sincerely believe you can do it, you can do it ... it's a great time to be an entrepreneur right now ... it doesn't take a whole lot of money to incorporate ... it doesn't take that much money to brand yourself and create a Web site ... The only other piece of advice I would give is do what you are good at ... stick fairly close to what you excel at ... also, get a small team of trusted mentors around you to advise you on areas in which you're not as well equipped."

Susan:

"You really need to be prepared to experience the fact that you're not going to have a regular paycheck and that takes a lot of getting used to ... when you're working for a company you are accustomed to regular income ... it's almost like a crutch ... when it isn't there it's very liberating, but at first it is also very scary ... I would also advise having some kind of financial safety net so that you won't feel terrified if you don't have any income for a period of time ... and if you are the kind of person who likes a social environment with a lot of people around you, it may not be the right life for you ... it can be very lonely."

Knowing that you don't want to continue working in a large corporation is one thing; working out what you want to do instead is something else. Most of the women I interviewed had explored three main areas of thinking:

1. What am I passionate about (or at least really interested in)?

2. Do I have the necessary skills and capabilities? If not, can I get them?

3. Is there a market for what I want to do?

The following two stories from Linda Ward O'Farrell and Zulma Guzman are great examples of women who are passionate about their businesses, have developed the skills they need to be successful and who have identified a gap in the market for what they offer. Through their own small companies both Linda and Zulma have become leaders in their own countries and professions in what they do.

Names

Linda Ward O'Farrell and **Zulma Guzman**

Former lives

Linda was a director of human resources at a national railway company.

Zulma worked with the Colombian government on environmental issues.

New lives

Linda has her own independent relocation consulting company (www.wardofarrell.com). In 2005 Linda received the Canadian Employee Relocation Council's President's Award for her outstanding contribution to the industry, where she is seen as a leader and somewhat of a guru.

Zulma has her own independent urban redevelopment consultancy in Bogota, Colombia, the first of this type of company in her country (www.urbia.com.co).

Motivation for change

Linda

"My company relocated their head office to Calgary and I didn't want to move … I decided to set up my own business rather than look for another corporate job because I was tired of a lot of what was going on within large corporations…. there are a lot of things that you do and redo that I didn't see the purpose of … also because of the number of hours I was putting in … I just needed a break and some peace and quiet for awhile and not spend my life running from meeting to meeting … I also wanted the flexibility to do other things that I enjoyed, like skiing, exercising, painting, drawing, being creative, doing charitable work, and spending time with my son."

Zulma

"There was an election and the government changed … the new government had different priorities … environmental issues were seen as a luxury … I left because I really felt that I was wasting my time and my talent … I moved to a small company doing something completely different for two years … then I became a mother and I started thinking differently. I just wanted to be with my son and have time to see him growing and not just keep working all of the time."

How they did it

Linda:

"I took a package from my company and started my business in 1996 ... about five years prior to this, I had identified a need in Canada for independent consulting in relocation ... no one was doing it and so I knew there was a need ... I gave myself a two-year plan and I thought, if it's not successful in two years I'll pound the pavement and find another job ... I didn't know if I would be self-motivated or have the entrepreneurial spirit because I had largely always been motivated by others ... I set up a home office, a dedicated space, so that it wouldn't creep into my home and my home wouldn't creep into my office ... then I just started work ... made some phone calls, started planning, writing the mandate, the vision, what I would and wouldn't do ... I had a lot of support in the industry because I had a really good network ... they assured me there was a need for someone like me."

Zulma

"My skills in environmental issues were not really of value here in Columbia and so many times I thought about leaving the country, but I have a husband here and so I tried to find jobs at international companies who might be interested in these issues, but it wasn't easy ... then I started thinking about my lost love of architecture ... I thought about training as an architect ... so I found a short summer course in New York to see if I had the talent ... I had never drawn or designed anything and so I didn't know if I had the skill ... I went there for two months of summer school, mainly with teenagers, and spent my days drawing and learning about architecture, and that was a lot of fun ... I learned that I wasn't really very good at it, but I discovered that what really made me happy was working with architects ... and so that's what I do now ... I set up my own urban renewal consultancy ... I put into practice all of my knowledge of environmental economics and I set up projects that recycle land ... I look around the city and find places that have deteriorated but have very good value because of where they are located ... I develop a strategic plan ... I look for investors and set up the financials ... I hire a lot of architects and set up and manage the teams ... From the beginning I worked with a friend of mine who is an architect because I really needed someone who could speak that language ... and I have two investors who own the company with me."

Challenges

Linda:

"There are days where it is lonely, especially before my colleagues Dina and John came on board ... I have few people to bounce ideas off and so it can be lonely. So you have to get out and meet people ... It also took me a long time to figure out how long it would take me to do a particular project ... I had never really thought in terms of how long it would take me to do something ... so there were hits and misses ... I had to learn a lot of things, like time management and putting together a proposal, putting something in writing that would really reflect who I am, what I do, how I think, what I can deliver ... I learned that I have comfort zones like getting lost in the analysis and not looking at the end product the way I should ... when you get caught in a comfort zone you've got no one else to pull you out ... you have to do it yourself."

Zulma:

"The work is very demanding because everything depends on me ... I have to spend a lot of time arranging meetings and business dinners ... but I still manage to arrange my schedule around my son, Mateo ... if I have to go to his school or go see him swimming that is a priority and I will work later into the night ... income is low right now because I am at the start ... but the future looks good ... the projects are huge and long term ... this is a whole new area in my country and I am just learning as I go along ... also in Columbia it is more difficult to do business as a woman ... you have to say everything twice to be heard ... you have to fight more to make things happen ... and the men I work with are not exactly politically correct ... in a corporate environment this is easier to manage because there are established rules … I deal with different types of harassment all the time."

Advantages

Linda:

"I love the freedom and flexibility of doing what I do when I want to do it … of choosing what I want to do and what I don't want to do … I have set a vision and a mandate and, if I don't want to work with a particular client, I really don't have to … I do work longer hours but they're different hours and they're my hours … I can be a lot more productive in a day because I don't have to attend meetings that are a waste of time … now that people pay me for meetings they need to be sure that there's a value to my being there … and when I had fifty-five employees, if I had two employees per day in my office with problems, that was very time consuming … I don't have to deal with that now."

Zulma:

"I am the first company in Colombia specializing in this type of work and therefore the competition and barriers to entry in my business are low … I enjoy the challenge … and unlike when I was working in the government I do not have to fight to get my ideas accepted … my husband always told me that I had to find my passion and I did not believe him … now I do … Bogota is a big and important city in Latin America and we should have a really nice and well-planned city and the private sector should be engaged in the developments and that's why I do what I do."

Advice

Linda:

"If you are thinking about doing it, just do it. Whatever the risks and perils, there's always the opportunity to go back into large organizations … the risk of not succeeding in one's business is the same as the risk of being terminated in a large corporation … I would say absolutely do it because you discover things about yourself and what you are actually able to do ... I think your sense of your own value changes."

Zulma:

"Being independent demands a lot of sacrifice, so if you decide to leave a comfortable and well-paid job, make sure it is for something you are passionate about ... you can bear the challenges of running your own business if you are following your passion and if your family is more important to you than being a corporate leader."

Transitioning from being an employee of a large organization to becoming self-employed can be very challenging. One way in which to make this move a little easier is to subcontract to a larger company. In this way you have the benefits of being self-employed, but someone else is doing the marketing and selling for you. Rebecca Stewart is one example of a woman who has taken this route and who is reaping the benefits.

Name

Rebecca Stewart

Previous life

Manager in an international financial services company in Australia

New life

International contract trainer based in the United Kingdom

Motivation for change

Rebecca's motivation for leaving both her company and her country was love. "I met my husband when he was out in Australia on a backpacking holiday. The holiday romance got serious and I chased him all the way back to England, throwing away my perfectly good job, my family, and my friends. And here I am eight years later ... once here I was doing some temporary work for a training company ... the opportunity came up to try doing some training and it seemed like an interesting challenge ... it had the best aspects of people management without all of the responsibility, so I thought I'd give it a try ... and so it all started with a sense of adventure and being open to new opportunities."

How she did it

"There are two broad business models for the type of training that I do. One, you can set up your own little company and do the sales and marketing and account management yourself, as well as deliver the work. Or, the model I am currently following, is to subcontract to larger, more established training companies who sort of act as my agent because they do the sales and marketing and account manage-ment ... I simply had to become accredited in various training products ... which means that I am licensed to deliver these workshops ... the reason that I opted for this business model is that I don't have a sales and marketing background ... and the prospect of doing marketing mail shots from my living room didn't excite me ... I also realized that as a small-business owner you have to be good at just about every-thing ... so this is really an off-the-shelf business model."

Challenges

"It took me about eighteen months to get over my alpha female side, relax into it, and try not to control the situation so much ... and I have to say it took me about three years to adequately establish my network, so that I no longer have to lose sleep about where the work is coming from ... because the work is network based there can be quite a time between initially setting up and having a full schedule ... the other thing is that you really do need to enjoy it because you're on your feet day-after-day when you are training and I don't think that it's for everyone."

Advantages

"I have complete flexibility of my schedule. I choose to work when I want to and so I have the opportunity for real work/life balance

... and, as I've said, I have the best aspects of people management without the boring stuff that comes with it ... and the advantage of working with licensed products is that they come with their very own established trainer networks ... so for two of the products I train we meet annually as trainers to ensure global consistency and share ideas ... which means trips to Thailand and Japan and other places where we work ... so I satisfy my need for a professional network that way ... I really enjoy it ... I work with organizations now and I see the problems and the concerns and the cultural issues that they have and I just feel lucky to be an outsider looking in."

Advice

"My advice would be to find something you are good at that you enjoy ... get good at it and work out how to make money at it ... there are many business models out there that are perfectly within one's realm of capability ... and build and use your network ... networking is critical for me ... I attend as many events as possible within my established network ... I also use LinkedIn and belong to speakers groups and things like that ... my advice would be to take every opportunity to build relationships."

Not everyone is cut out to be self-employed or an entrepreneur. A different route out of large, traditional organizations is to join and lead a much smaller company where you have more control and autonomy to create the corporate culture that you want. Some high-profile female executives have made the news for doing just this. In 2008 Julia Reynolds, the highest-ranking woman in Tesco's £1 billion clothing operation (Tesco is one of the world's leading retailers), traded in her job to run the much smaller online lingerie retailer, Figleaves.com. When she left her large corporation she publically condemned the macho posturing she believes is common in U.K. boardrooms, saying she was fed up with working alongside "chest-beating alpha males ... there are lots of people trying to get out of big corporations ... they want the fulfillment and job satisfaction that corporates can't provide."[98]

Like Julia Reynolds, other female executives are opting-out of large corporations to express their business and leadership capabilities in smaller arenas. May Scally and Susan Cordts are two women I met who had had big jobs in very large organizations, but chose to use their expertise and experience to lead much smaller companies, where they now have more flexibility and control in creating the organizational values and culture in which they thrive.

Names

May Scally and **Susan Cordts**

Former lives

May was formerly a vice president of electronic marketing at a major telecommunications company in Canada.

Susan was formerly a vice president in a large healthcare organization, then in a large pharmaceutical company in the USA.

Both ran departments in these organizations that were bigger than the entire companies that they now lead.

New lives

May is currently general manager and 20 percent owner of Labplas (www.labplas.com), a privately owned manufacturing company based in Quebec, Canada.

Susan is now president and CEO of Adaptive Technologies Inc. (www.adaptiveinc.com), a privately owned business intelligence and predictive analytics business based in Phoenix, Arizona.

Motivation for change

Both May and Susan had spent years working their way up the corporate ladder and had very successful careers that could have continued in a traditional, large corporate setting. They had professional credibility, status, and big paychecks. Many people thought they were crazy to give it up—and so why did they?

May:

"I loved my job until I became a VP at corporate where I found I had far less control over my environment and I was confronted on a daily basis with tons of politics. As a vice president in a large corporation, you have absolutely no authority over anything. I had no control over the projects I worked on and found myself, for the first time in my career, working on something I didn't believe in and which couldn't succeed. It was a seven-day–a-week job, which was OK, but when I did my own time-and-motion study, I realized I was spending over 60 percent of my time pulling together presentation decks, which were probably not read most of the time and thrown in the garbage. I definitely need to work in an environment where I can make my own decisions and work on something I believe in."

Susan:

"Both the hospitals and the pharmaceutical company where I worked were very large organizations and eventually I found that my vision and values around patient care were not in alignment with those of the organization. There was a lot of talk about who we were and what we stood for, but actions often didn't align with the talk. There was no longer a fit for me and I needed to do something different."

How they did it

May:

May turned down the next job she was offered—a VP marketing position in another division of the same organization, because she "just didn't see the match anymore." She negotiated a severance package and left the organization with no clear plan or alternative job to go to. She then spent the next year applying for other corporate positions, looking for an organizational environment where "the decision making was perhaps more truthful, more direct, and a little less about politics." When this didn't work out she quickly moved toward exploring other industries through taking small consulting mandates that exposed her to different types of companies and different organizational environments. During this experimental stage, where she also did lots of reading and "testing things out," she consulted to Lablas, a small manufacturing organization where she did such a good job that the owner asked her to take over leading the organization. Six years down the road, May is now a 20 percent owner and has led the company through very challenging times from a $4 million to a $6 million company. She has expanded her markets, streamlined and improved processes, improved staff retention, created her own organizational culture, and dramatically improved her own quality of life.

Susan:

After resigning her job at a large pharmaceutical company and subsequently starting and then leaving a business venture where her values were again out of alignment with those of her business partners, Susan was offered the opportunity to lead Adaptive Technologies, Inc., a small privately held company of five board members, eight shareholders and twenty-five employees. Having experienced a clash of values in her previous organizations, Susan has, over the last seven years, been able to grow the company and create her own organizational culture where "everything is about relationship rather than transactions." She has expanded the business through external collaborations and created a "fun and exciting culture that values people and allows them to grow and prosper ... we are about excellence and we are about respect ... .excellence in terms of how we service our customers and in how we encourage our employees to take risks in search of more excellence ... and we have a big core value around respecting our customers and respecting each other internally. Everyone joining or collaborating with our company has to understand and align with this core value of respect."

Challenges

May:

"The biggest thing for me to get over was not that I would be earning less money; it was more about my ego and identity. I had identified with the company for so many years and there was a lot of prestige associated with the position I had. It was a door opener in many ways—in many social and professional circles. My identity was tied in with this in subtle and unknown ways. During my transition year I realized that what was bothering me most was that I was cutting off a part of me and killing a part of my identity for good. If any doors were going to open in the future, it would be because of me and would have nothing to do with my past position and status. During this phase of my transition, it was my biggest point of insecurity ... there comes a day when you have to put your ego aside ... and if you can still feel the same sense of self-worth that you felt before, if you can truly understand that your corporate position is not what makes you who you are ... then you don't need any other security."

Susan:

"I have a lot more stress than I had before because I have people that I'm responsible for ... to make sure that they are provided for ... that they get a repeated paycheck and that they have opportunities to grow. Another challenge is that in large organizations you have a sense, probably a false sense, of more security in that every employee doesn't have to walk around thinking about how he or she individually contributes to revenue ... you perhaps have more of a sense of security by being lost in the masses."

Advantages

May:

"I think one of the biggest successes of my new career is having created an extremely open culture that is at the same time extremely performance-based ... everyone knows what everyone else is working on and if there is someone not pulling his or her weight, I don't even have to get involved—they handle it among themselves ... People also have different circumstances and everyone here gets what they need ... it is not an egalitarian culture ... if you have young children, or aging parents, or you are a young person attending university part-time, you have different needs ... and we work it out so that we each get what we need ... there's no backstabbing or bickering and very little comparing and bitching."

Susan:

"I have a lot more control over my life now than I had before and, even though I work at least as hard, if not harder, I am in control of how I spend my time ... no one else is telling me what to do or how I must spend my time ... I still have stress but it's now much more productive stress."

Advice

May:

"If you are in a large corporate environment and you're starting to feel like a slave; you feel like you have no choice; you feel like you must constantly be checking your voicemail and your BlackBerry; you feel like work is driving you rather than you driving it—if you have any of these symptoms you have a problem that you need to face, either on your own or with the help of friends or an executive coach ... and it's important before you make any change to dissect and understand your fears and to figure out what you really want."

Susan:

"One of the main reasons people are hesitant about changing careers is because they lack self-confidence. You need to surround yourself with people who are positive influences and who believe in you and who give you honest feedback to help you understand your strengths and weaknesses ... to help you embrace your strengths and overcome your weaknesses and feel empowered to enable you to drive forward. I think that when you feel that sense of empowerment and people believe in you, you feel like you can drive forward and make the change."

Some women who described their stories to me had made more dramatic changes and left corporations and the business world altogether to find more meaning in their lives and their work. I was fortunate enough to be introduced to three such women who all combined their love of travel with a desire to help those less fortunate than themselves.

Names

Stephanie Faubert, **Ton Berg,** and **Marilyn McHarg**

Former lives

Stephanie was a senior consultant and manager in technology at a major consulting firm.

Ton was a sales and marketing director for an international organization.

Marilyn was acting nursing director in an intensive care unit.

New lives

All now work as part of Médecins Sans Frontières (MSF), an international humanitarian aid organization that provides emergency medical assistance to populations in danger in more than seventy countries. In other parts of the world, you might know this organization as Doctors Without Borders.

Motivation for change

Stephanie:

"I loved the work as a management consultant and had a successful career but it started to feel a little one-dimensional for me. I was very focused on my work and I wasn't paying much attention to my other interests or parts of my life. Work was good, but life was unfulfilling.

"The changes for me were triggered by a series of things. A motivational speaker that the firm had engaged to motivate the management team was the catalyst for me to take some time away from work to get some rest and clarity about my life. I took six months' leave of absence and traveled alone in parts of the Mediterranean, Middle East, and a little bit of Africa. When I returned, one of my closest friends was diagnosed with a terminal cancer. We talked a lot and I felt that I needed to make the most of the opportunities that I had—life is short. So I decided to quit the firm and accept an offer from an overland travel company in Africa to be an overland safari guide.

"I didn't want to look back and think,'Wow, I really should have done that and now I can't because my circumstances have changed.' I knew I wouldn't be doing it forever, but I wanted to do it for a year."

Ton:

"The company where I had been working for a long time asked me to take on responsibility for the rest of the world, as well as Europe. When I thought about it, I realized that it was really more of the same with even more travel and being away from home ... and so I decided instead to try something completely different ... I took a job that involved reorganizing a city public transport system ... I had no clue about public transport ... and the job started with 350 drivers protesting against my appointment ... but it ended up a really nice job ... they knew everything about public transport but nothing about managing an organization and we were very complementary ... they valued the different expertise that I brought ... after this I realized that if I could manage something so completely different to anything I'd done before, maybe I could jump into something really, really, different ... I built up twenty years of good management experience and I always enjoy trying something different and I wanted to see if I could use my experience to work on other issues in completely different settings, which MSF allows me to do."

Marilyn:

"I was having dinner with a friend of mine, Dr. Richard Heinzl, who was looking to bring MSF, which already existed in Europe, over to

Canada. He talked to me about the principles and the values of the organization and it really pulled me in ... the idea of being able to help people and make a difference ... the way that doctors and nurses go off to these really difficult places and make a difference in their patients' lives ... I was just very taken by it and decided to get involved."

How they did it

Stephanie:

Stephanie resigned and took a job as an overland guide based in Zimbabwe. Even though she had no experience in this work, they offered her the job because of her independent travel experience and her relative maturity (Stephanie was in her early thirties. Most of their guides, and many of the clients, were ten years younger). They recognized that her age and organizational experience as a management consultant would enable her to manage groups of people and deal with whatever came along. "The skills that you need to be a decent overland guide are not so different from the skills you need to be a good management consultant or project manager. The team dynamics, managing a group of twenty-four people night and day for eight weeks ... making sure that despite differing motivations, you want to make sure that everyone is satisfied with what they get from the experience. Managing time constraints, financial constraints, navigating obstacles, having very good communication skills and the ability to arbitrate disagreements. It was a huge amount of work, but very fulfilling and one of the best experiences of my life ... once I had this experience, I felt like I could do anything. I realized that the skills and experience that I had could be of value beyond narrowly defined consulting or project management in a corporate environment."

After a year of this work and a couple of episodes of malaria, Stephanie knew that, if she wanted to stay current and marketable in the field of technology, she had to get back to that kind of work. She returned to Toronto and established herself as an independent consultant with the idea that it would provide more flexibility and she could do other things in between contracts.

Her love of Africa and her desire to get back there led her to find out more about MSF. "I was thinking about how to get back to Africa and what organizations I could work with where I could get more than a superficial understanding of what was happening there. I was also hoping that I could invest more of my time and skills there, rather than just traveling through. I did some research and investigated MSF. I really liked what I read about them and their principles and values ... and so I got in touch with them in the hope that I had some skills that would match a nonmedical role in the organization. I rented out my place in Toronto and went with MSF for a year in central Asia ... I worked for a couple of months in logistics and then I became a project coordinator in Turkmenistan.... I loved it ... it was a very educational and humbling experience ... I thought that I could alternate my work as a management consultant with work overseas with MSF."

Ton:

"One month per year I would travel to Africa on vacation and I always thought it would be great if I could just work for a year there and see if I could transfer all of my corporate experience in a different setting ... everyone in Holland knows of MSF, they are very well respected and I knew a few people who worked there because a lot of people join them and do one or two missions ... I thought it would be great to join them, but I am not a doctor or a financial expert and so I didn't think they would be interested in me ... by coincidence I heard from a friend that they were looking for people and so I got in contact with them and we agreed that I would work for them for one year in Africa as head of mission, which means that I am responsible for MSF projects in that country or region ... that was back in 1994 ... and today I am still here ... I started as head of mission for projects in Somalia and now I am back in Ethiopia managing projects near where I started in 1994 ... since '94 most of my life has been in Africa ... five years in the Congo but also time in the Sudan, Palestine, Angola, and quite a few other places ... it can be extremely frustrating working in war zones where you are trying to help people and save lives, but then you realize that if we didn't do this these people would have no assistance and support ... it's not just about giving them medicines but also about showing them that they are not completely abandoned and that people still care about what is happening to them."

Marilyn:

"After signing on with MSF, I decided that I really wanted to do at least one mission and so I went as a field nurse to Uganda for a year. This was at a time when Uganda was just starting to stabilize after quite a long war. Then when I finished that assignment, I realized that this wasn't done for me and I did more assignments in North Sudan, South Sudan, and Liberia ... I've been with MSF for seventeen years now and during that time I have also worked at MSF headquarters in Holland and Geneva ... during this time I have not only made use of my nursing skills and experience, but have had tremendous growth in terms of my management and leadership abilities."

Challenges

Stephanie:

Stephanie has created a life where she alternates between consulting contracts and MSF missions.

"One downside to alternating between consulting and my work with MSF is that it's not necessarily what the corporate world recognizes as relevant experience, at least until it's discussed in some detail ... when I look for work after having been away for some time, I sometimes get offered a lower rate of pay, given the fact that I've been out of circulation for a while."

Ton:

"One challenge is that, when you are on a mission, you spend much more time with your team than you would with corporate teams ... In this kind of work you work together, eat together, and live together ... You can't go home in the evening and have your own private life ... It's a much more intense way of living and working together. But it's also a very good way to coach people because there is more time and opportunity."

Marilyn:

"One of the biggest challenges has to be trying to provide a level of health care under really austere circumstances ... Also working and living with the teams ... when you are on a field mission with MSF, you live and breathe the work ... And the working conditions and the insecurity can be pretty tough ... Getting some balance in my life is also a challenge, which has been one of my motivations to come back to Canada to be closer to my family ... I'm a bit of a work-in-progress on this point."

Advantages

Stephanie:

"One of the great things about doing work with MSF is that you meet a lot of like-minded people—people who engage in real discussion and debate about the bigger picture in the world and our roles, both collectively and as individuals in it."

Ton:

"When I was doing corporate work I didn't really think about it ... But now I know I really am making a difference to peoples' lives ... I am using the same skills as a manager in a corporation to facilitate and manage projects, but the projects are about life and death ... And people really appreciate you for it ... I've also learned to appreciate much more the life we live ... it makes me a little more humble and more grateful ... It has made me more of a spokes-person for doing things that contribute in whatever small way to peoples' lives."

Marilyn:

"It's the act of being able to help people and make a difference with others who really need it. It's not an easy job, but it's a very rewarding one ... and being exposed to so many different cultures and meeting so many great people around the world has been a real pleasure."

Advice

Stephanie:

"Find some clarity ... take time to reflect and try to understand yourself and your values ... you have to figure out what's most important to you before you can make it happen. And live your life."

Ton:

"When I left corporate business, quite a few people I had been working with said they were jealous and that they would love to do what I was doing ... so my advice is to just do it ... you can always go back ... your corporate skills won't disappear."

Marilyn:

"Try taking a step back and make sure you have a good perspective on what you are doing; if you are really dissatisfied look at other alternatives that may be more rewarding in your life ... the bottom line is that we spend so many hours at work it's got to be something that really grabs you on some level."

After returning from Burma, Stephanie has established a life where she divides her time between working as an independent consultant in the technology industry and taking projects in various countries with MSF. Currently she has been back in Toronto for a couple of years and is yet to decide if she will take another mission with MSF.

After spending the first two years in Africa alone Ton and her life partner created possibilities for him to join her. She has worked with MSF as head of mission for the past fifteen years, occasionally taking breaks to return to Holland for rest and recuperation. When I interviewed Ton, she spoke to me from her office in the Somali region in Ethiopia.

After years in the field with MSF, Marilyn returned to Toronto to be closer to her family and to establish a Canadian operational desk supervising MSF activities in five different countries. She currently holds the position of general director.

Stephanie, Ton, and Marilyn successfully transferred their skills from the private sector to the nonprofit world. Moving from the private sector to the nonprofit sector is one option for men or women who are looking for a different working environment. Currently, there is a leadership gap in nonprofit organizations, largely due to baby boomer retirements, but also because nonprofit organizations are increasing in size and complexity and new roles are being created. Transitioning from the private to the nonprofit sector can be tricky, particularly in terms of cultural fit. But more and more nonprofit organizations are valuing private sector leadership and management experience. The following stories from Judy McLeod and Francoise Gagnon are examples of women who have successfully made this transition.

Names

Judy McLeod and **Francoise Gagnon**

Previous lives

Judy was an executive vice president, operations, at a national technology communications company.

Francoise was a senior director of public affairs at a national telecommunications company.

New lives

Judy is now executive vice president for operations for the YMCA of Greater Toronto, a charity focused on community support and development.

Francoise started as executive director of Equal Voice, a nonprofit organization devoted to the "still-bold idea" that more women must be elected to every level of government in Canada. She has now transitioned to leading a mentorship program for young girls in the same organization.

Motivation for change

Judy:

"For the first time in my life I found myself in a space where I really didn't see what I would do next, I didn't have a goal ... I didn't have aspirations to become president and that was really the only job left for me to reach for and it just didn't appeal to me ... then my husband was diagnosed with a serious illness that would get progressively worse over time ... when you're in the executive track in the corporate world the reality is it is fourteen-hour days ... you're grinding it out day in and day out ... and the thing that always kept me going was having the next goal that I wanted to get to ... I didn't have that anymore and we didn't know how long my husband was going to be well ... and so I decided to leave."

Francoise:

"The telecom industry was about to go through some significant changes ... and my role was about to change to one that I had done fairly extensively before and I really did not want to go back to that type of job ... I felt like I had been there and done that."

How they did it

Judy:

Judy took a year off and traveled with her husband, while his health was still good enough. "The thing I realized after a year away was that I really enjoyed the flexibility ... I had been on that work-home-work-home treadmill for so many years that I never actually thought about it being any different." On her return she was offered another big corporate job, but when she reflected on it, she realized that "the notion of going back to an office every day was just making me ill. I just couldn't imagine doing it

... and so I turned down the offer." Judy was eventually attracted to join a small, elite consulting company of former C-level executives that helped match entrepreneurs with sources of capital and other business services. This was a job that still allowed her the flexibility of spending time with her husband and pursuing other adventures, such as going to Africa with a group of sixteen women and climbing Mount Kilimanjaro. "While I was there I had a lot of time to think. It was ten days up-and-down that mountain and then eight days on safari with sixteen other women. So there was lots of time to reflect and talk and cry and all those things women do when they are together ... during this time I decided I was going to leave the consulting business ... Even though I liked the flexibility, I never felt I had a real passion for it ... even though my clients loved me and several had tried to hire me, it just wasn't work I felt a great deal of satisfaction for." Judy wasn't sure what she wanted to do next, but the one thing she was sure of was "I didn't want to go back to the corporate world ... I felt I had served my sentence of delivering value to shareholders and I wasn't interested in that anymore ... it just didn't turn me on ... I still wanted to work in a large organization but I was hoping it could be an organization where I could effect change for good on a large scale ... maybe a not-for-profit but I wasn't sure about that. Most of the Canadian not-for-profits aren't really big enough to fit my criteria."

Judy explored her thinking with friends and trusted advisors with no real idea of where this would lead. Exactly eight hours out of hospital after some elective surgery she was contacted by a search firm looking to fill the position of chief operating officer for the YMCA. "I was interested and did some research ... I didn't know much about the YMCA and thought they were more about gym, swim, and summer camps ... I had no idea of the social mission work they do. And so the more research I did the more I got hooked. And then I met some people there and really liked them and, as it turned out, they really liked me too. I got a job offer in December 2008 and started at the end of January 2009."

Francoise:

"I looked at other options and this job came up at Equal Voice ... I had originally come from a nonprofit background ... and the beauty of working in a small organization and certainly a not-for-profit organization, is you get to play all roles by virtue of the fact that typically there aren't a lot of resources. So you get to be fundraiser, chief operating officer, CEO, and everything else in between, and I liked the flexibility that offered."

Challenges

Judy:

"The YMCA is a large complex not-for-profit ... thirty-five hundred employees and a budget of $150 million ... a very engaged board of business leaders ... most of the issues we talk about are the same ones I talked about in the private sector ... I think for many people who are thinking of taking the route I took from the private to the not-for-profit sector it can be a harsh transition ... I got some great advice from others who had already made this transition ... some people thought that going from the private sector to the not-for-profit sector would drive me crazy, because it was less well-organized and not well-funded ... they didn't think I would do well in this type of environment ... the YMCA is about as corporate as you can get for a not-for-profit but there are some significant differences ... the YMCA is an international organization but it's also a federation ... there's no centralized power, so things have to be done through collaboration with members, volunteers, and staff ... I think women adapt well to this because we manage differently and we are more often open to collaboration. So it's not been a hard transition, but it is different."

Francoise:

"I don't really have any resources ... so I have to do everything from printing out labels to running to the post office ... so I get to do all the grunt work ... but every job has its challenges and I can learn to print labels ... I manage."

Advantages

Judy:

One of the things Judy was looking for in her next career was something she could feel passionate about. She spoke with great passion about the work she is now involved in.

"The work we do is very exciting; for example, we run a small alternative school for high school kids with learning disabilities ... grades nine to twelve ... it's very small at the moment and we're figuring out how to expand it ... some of these kids had substance-abuse problems, learning problems—they had really checked out of the school system and their parents were frustrated beyond belief ... right now there's about fifty-five kids in the school and twelve of them are graduating ... of these twelve, two are now published poets and two have been recognized by Adobe, the software company ... they ran an international competition for videos produced by young people and two of our students were selected ... in fact, one of them is getting international recognition and is going to Geneva this year to get involved in the editing project ... the notion that we can affect the lives of these young people is amazing ... 100 percent of our students have graduated over the five years the school has been running ... they are either continuing on to university or they have jobs ... it's an incredible success story ... and this is just a small example of the work we do and I have this stuff going on every day ... what's not to like about it ... it's not about delivering value to shareholders and dealing with greedy people who just want to wring the last dollar out of what you're doing. So it's quite lovely ... the last five years has completely changed my perspective ... I now try to live every moment and I try to make every day special ... I go to bed at night and try to think of at least one thing that day that to me was amazing ... helping others is a very powerful motivator ... I grew up in a small town where helping others came naturally ... getting back to my roots feels really good."

Francoise:

After successfully establishing the role of executive director of Equal Voice, Francoise handed over that job to someone else and created a new role for herself as senior program director of a mentoring program for young women.

"I'm working on a program that targets young girls between the ages of twelve to twenty-five, and absolutely loving it. This is not something I would have had the opportunity to do in the private sector. I'm very passionate about the program and the potential we have for growing it ... I also enjoy the lack of bureaucracy and the opportunity to do a bit of everything ... on any given day I could be doing anything from fundraising, to writing, to being out networking ... I just get involved in everything from the ground up."

Francoise has an unusual blend of private and nonprofit experience. When her current project ends in 2011 she is unsure what she will do next, but is attracted by the idea of creating some kind of consultancy that utilizes her experience. One thing she is sure about is that "it would take a lot to get me back into the grind of corporate life."

Advice

Judy:

"If you are able to, take some time off. Taking a year off really helped me ... I had been going at ninety-miles-per-hour for over thirty years ... if I had left my job and jumped straight into something else, I would probably have jumped into something exactly like I was already doing and I'd still be on the same track instead of where I am today ... so take time off and reflect and experience new ways of living ... Also build and tap into your network ... I had what I call my personal board of advisors ... men and women who were great sounding boards for me ... I have also found that expanding the circle of people I know to be an invaluable resource and it's been worth every second to me ... it's taken me into the lives of women that I wouldn't have otherwise crossed paths with and that's been fabulous."

Francoise:

"Check your ego at the door because it is often the corporate position that others are interested in rather than your own personal attributes ... work out what it is you want in life and don't be put off by the skeptics."

Yet another option when leaving the corporate world is to teach what you know. I met two Canadian lawyers who have changed careers by expanding and applying their expertise within their discipline, but in a completely different setting. Law firms are infamous for their macho working environments of long hours and inflexible working arrangements,—two of the main reasons why so many talented women lawyers resign their jobs to pursue careers with more flexibility. The Law Society of Upper Canada has described the "lawyer culture" as one that has almost been developed to exclude women. The assumption has been that "a lawyer would not have family responsibilities requiring significant time commitments" and that "women were expected to take responsibility for all of the domestic labour arising out of family responsibilities. The hidden corollary to these assumptions was that women would not be lawyers."[99]

Names

Catherine Piche and **Maude Choko**

Former lives

Lawyers

New lives

Catherine is currently studying for her doctorate in law at McGill University and is now a law professor at the University of Montreal.

Maude is currently studying for her doctorate in law at McGill University and has started teaching at the University of Montreal as a lecturer. She is also acting in films and plays.

Motivation for change

Catherine:

"I worked for about six years in law firms in New York and Montreal doing litigation work.... When my first child was born I decided to leave and go back to school to do a doctorate degree ... my life as a lawyer was high-powered, interesting, and stimulating ... but also very stressful and very long hours ... I also found that I was delegating the research and writing work that I was really interested in ... I like mentoring and working with others and this aspect was also lacking in my work as a lawyer."

Maude:

"When I became pregnant with my first child, it was not well received in my law firm ... after returning from my pregnancy leave, I continued to work for about eight months and then I decided to leave ... my husband is also a lawyer and we found it impossible for us both to work that hard and have kids."

How they did it

Catherine:

"I decided to go back to school and study for my doctorate in law ... the idea was to change careers within the law ... from a law firm to an academic job ... and the way to do that was essentially to focus exclusively on the doctoral project and writing, publishing, and attending conferences ... it worked out really well, even though I have two young boys at home ... I was able to achieve my goal and I have just gotten a position at the University of Montreal as a law professor."

Maude:

"I didn't know exactly what I would do or if I would completely stop practicing law ... I was clear that I couldn't stay at a big law firm ... but I wasn't exactly clear about what I would do after ... I completed a master's degree in law that I had started when I was pregnant with my first child and then had a second baby ... and I felt like going back to what I liked doing before I went into law ... and so I took some acting classes ... as a result, I have been participating in different film projects as an actor. I have even produced some projects of my own ... last September I presented a play that ran for two weeks ... I am also doing my doctorate in law right now and my goal is to teach law and to be able to have a balance with doing some work in theater and cinema ... I want to create a balance between teaching and acting ... at this point I'm not interested in choosing between them because I really think they could be compatible careers in some way."

Challenges

Catherine:

"The first challenge was obviously economic ... it's significant to go from a lawyer's salary to being a student ... another challenge was getting myself organized and being self-motivated to set goals and then go for them ... when you are working at home you are your own boss ... it can be hard juggling kids and working from home ... there was also a little bit of a stigma attached to what I was doing ... people were asking why I was doing this and thinking I was absolutely crazy ... leaving a stable, well-paid job in anticipation that I might one day get a job in a completely different organization ... but it wasn't that risky because I knew I could always go back and find a job in a law firm."

Maude:

"It was hard on my self-esteem at the beginning because I wasn't sure what I was going to do and I wasn't sure how other people were going to judge me ... but I am way past that now ... sometimes I have a hard time defining myself ... depending on who I am talking to I will say I am a doctoral student or an actress ... I don't fit into a neat category for people ... I've accepted this for myself but it's hard to explain to others."

Advantages

Catherine:

"I particularly enjoy the flexibility in terms of how I organize and do my work ... I also enjoy my new way of leading within the university ... I have a special role with the students ... I'm like a role model, a teacher, and a bit like a friend and so it's a special kind of relationship ... we are very happy because changing careers has really worked out for me."

Maude:

"I'm not stressed anymore ... once you realize that you're not in the right place I think it can be really harmful in the long term to continue for the wrong reasons ... I am also happier now because I simply enjoy every day of my life ... I actually have the time to live it and to be with my kids."

Advice

Catherine:

"When you wake up in the morning, if you don't want to go to work or you're not excited by what you do, you should definitely think about doing something else ... you need to set some goals and take some chances ... it's hard work but it's worth it."

Maude:

"The first step is to take some time off and think about what you really want to do ... then whatever plan you come up with stick with it for at least a couple of years ... and then take some more time out to step back and think and see where you are."

If people are unhappy in their work, it is usually to everyone's advantage that something changes. All of the women in this final section have made significant changes in order to feel happier and more fulfilled in their work and their lives. Cara Vogl, our final story, decided that she needed to jump off the high board and change almost every aspect of her life. If any of you have read the excellent book *Eat, Pray, Love* by Elizabeth Gilbert you might find some parallels in this story.

Name

Cara Vogl

Former life

Director of public relations for a large clothing retail company

New life

Traveler and budding writer

Motivation for change

"I was feeling bored and indifferent about my job at the company I had been with for fifteen years—on a treadmill of sorts. It is a wonderful company that gave me every opportunity to grow, but I felt like I was sleepwalking through my life. I was caught in the vicious cycle of making a certain amount of money to pay for the mortgage, the car, and buying things in an attempt to somehow fill this empty void. I had an increasingly sinking feeling and I didn't realize that I was the one in charge of doing something about it. I thought and hoped that one day something would just "happen" and then I realized that the only person who was trapping me was myself, through my fear. The only way that I could see myself getting out of this was to face the fear, wipe the slate clean, and start over."

How she did it

Cara decided that what she really wanted to do was to travel, get new experiences, and see where life took her. She quit her job, sold her house, put her possessions into storage, paid off her debts, put some money aside for a deposit on a new property, and used the rest of her money to travel the world.

"I bought a backpack and a one-way ticket to Zagreb and decided to travel until either I didn't like it anymore or the money ran out ... I ended up being away for seven months ... I stomped grapes in Croatia, I watched the sunrise over the Taj Mahal in India, I floated around in the sea in Greece, I went fishing for my dinner in Indonesia, and I spent New Year's eve in a tiny village in Laos ... I learned to live in the moment ... My goal was to feel something and I felt every second of every minute of every day, like I hadn't felt anything for years ... I ended up on a tiny island of fifteen hundred people in Indonesia where there is no electricity and no motorized vehicles and I just fell in love with it. I lived there for six weeks and ended up buying a piece of land ... so the money I put aside for a down payment on a new house in Canada, instead went to buy me a little piece of paradise covered with coconut trees and with an ocean breeze ... it seemed like a much better alternative."

During her travels Cara indulged her passion for writing and kept in touch with her friends and family back home by posting a blog about her experiences, her thoughts and her feelings. You can read this blog at www.travelpod.com/members/packingitin and her current blog since returning to Canada at http://ifiredme.blogspot.com.

Challenges

After seven months, when the money ran out, Cara returned to Canada, the happy owner of a piece of paradise in Indonesia, but with no job and no home. At the time of writing this book, she is living with her family, pursuing freelance work and figuring out how to earn enough money to support the new life that she is creating.

"I need some time to accept the fact that it's OK that I'm still searching and to be quiet and think and let things come to me. This is the hardest part that requires the most bravery. It wasn't quitting my job or selling the house that was the most difficult.... it's resisting the pressure to step back into old habits and an old way of life that is equated with stability and comfort. It's a big challenge to deal with the negative self-talk that I should know what to do next and I should be getting back to work ... it really requires a lot of boldness and bravery and that's where I am right now ... sometimes it's easier to know what you don't want and so I know that I don't want to go back to Monday-to-Friday, nine-to-five corporate life ... I'm not afraid to work hard but I want to work hard at something that means something to me now."

Advantages

"I am a changed person ... the experiences I had and the bravery and boldness of the incredible people that I met along the way have opened my eyes and made me feel connected in a much bigger way to something much more than chasing a dollar every day ... I have a tremendous sense of self and pride. I still can't believe that I did it ... if little me from London, Ontario, Canada, can do it, anyone can do it ... the only person who can change your life is you ... it's like I was dead and now I'm alive ... I was dulled to what was going on in the world and in my life. We tend to keep ourselves busy with day-to-day activities so that we don't have to ask ourselves the tough questions. So it's very easy to let years go by and never look inward. But once you do it's so freeing.

"I lamented the fact that I was single and not married for years, but now I realize it's like the universe was playing a joke on me. Now I think, thank goodness I'm single; otherwise, I would never have been able to do this ... I almost consider it a blessing ... I don't expect people to sell their homes and take the really drastic measures that I took ... that's what I needed for my life and my situation ... there are different ways to do it ... I met entire families who were traveling ... I met a couple who had taken their ten-year-old twins out of school to travel around the world for a year ... it doesn't have to be travel or selling your home ... just do something, no matter how small or seemingly insignificant, that scares you and makes you feel alive."

Advice

"It sounds really basic but go with what feels right in your gut ... the changes I have made have all felt right in my gut ... the way that I was living my life before, something always felt off ... there was always this little sinking feeling because, I realize now, I wasn't being true to myself ... and when you feel yourself backsliding, try to remind yourself why you're doing this ... get some perspective and remember your ultimate goal ... life is short and it is going by at the speed of light ... on my deathbed I won't be looking back and saying, 'I wish I had never quit that job where I was bored and taken that trip around the world' ... but I could have looked back and regretted that I didn't ... you'll never regret taking steps toward your own happiness, but you will regret the contrary ... it's like climbing to the top of a high diving board; if you look down for too long you're not going to jump ... so just get up there, walk to the end, and don't think about it—just jump."

These stories are a small selection of the many "corporate refugees" interviewed for this book. Although all of the women have different stories, common themes unite them. Most, if not all, felt some level of fear or apprehension before leaving the relative security of their corporate jobs, but none allowed it to stand in the way of creating a different life. Many talked of the importance of finding and pursuing their passions, alongside aligning their work with their values, and how this makes the long hours and hard work worthwhile and enjoyable. And all particularly enjoy the freedom and flexibility to design their days around what they think is important, rather than being confined by the demands of a corporate structure.

The message here is not that these alternative career paths are better than corporate careers, but simply that they are better for some people. Some of us thrive in large corporations and others increasingly feel like we are dying a slow death. The point is that we nearly always have a choice, even when it doesn't feel that way. If you are experiencing a deepening dissatisfaction with your life and your career, I would strongly agree with what many of these women recommend: take a break, get some distance and perspective, get support from your family, friends, and network and make some changes. As Cara Vogl says, "You will never regret taking steps toward your own happiness."

For more stories of corporate refugees go to www.unwritten rulesthebook.com

About the Author

Lynn Harris is an organizational development consultant and executive coach. She works with individuals, teams and organizations internationally; and she lives in Montreal, Canada, with her husband, Jeff, and her son, Josh. You can contact her through the Unwritten Rules website at www.unwrittenrulesthebook.com.

Endnotes

Chapter one

1. Clymer, A. "Book Says Nixon Considered a Woman for Supreme Court," *New York Times*, September 27, 2001, A16. http://query.nytimes.com/gst/fullpage.html?res=9B02EED6103AF934A1575A C0A9679C8B63&sec=&spon=&pagewanted=1.

2. Bowman, G.W., N.B. Worthy, and S.A. Greyser. "Are women executives people?" *Harvard Business Review 43* (1965) 4:14.

3. Hymowitz, C., and T.C. Schellhardt. "The glass ceiling: Why women can't seem to break the invisible barrier that blocks them from top jobs." *Wall Street Journal*, March 24, 1986. Special Supplement, 1, 4.

4. Hymowitz, C. "Through the glass ceiling." *Wall Street Journal*, November 8, 2004, R1, R3.

5. 2007/2008 United Nations Human Development Report. Gender Empowerment Measure. http://hdrstats.undp.org/en/indicators/282.html.

6. Catalyst, 2005 Catalyst Census of Women Board Directors (2006) and Catalyst, 2007 Census: Board Directors (2007).

7. Catalyst, 2005 Catalyst Census of Women Corporate Officers and Top Earners (2006) and Catalyst, 2007 Census: Corporate Officers and Top Earners (2007).

8. Catalyst, 2007 Catalyst Census of Women Board Directors of the FP500 (2008).

9. Rosenzweig & Co. "Report on women at the top levels of corporate Canada," 2009, www.rosenzweigco.com.

10. "EuropeanPWN Board Women," *Monitor* 2004, 2006, 2008

11. Center for American Women and Politics, Eagleton Institute of Politics, Rutgers. http://www.cawp.rutgers.edu/.

12. Women in national parliaments. http://www.ipu.org/wmn-e/classif.htm.

13. American Council on Education, The American College President 2007 (2007)

14. U.S. National Centers for Education Statistics. Digest of education statistics, 2005. http://nces.ed.gov/programs/digest/d05_df.asp.

15. Committee of 200, 2002, p. 17. The executive if Connie K. Duckworth, partner in 8 Wings Enterprises.

16. Pinker, Susan. "Fishing for Female Directors? Try Fresh Waters," *The Globe and Mail*, July 1, 2009.

17. Wood, W. and Eagly, A.H. "A cross-cultural analysis of the behavior of women and men: Implications for the origins of sex differences." *Psychological Bulletin* (2002), 128: 699-727

18. Eagly, Alice, H. and Carli, Linda, L. *Through the Labyrinth: the truth about how women become leaders* (Harvard Business School Press, 2007)

19. Sellers, P. and Mero, J. "Power: Do Women Really Want It?" *Fortune Magazine*, October 13, 2003. http://money.cnn.com/magazines/fortune/fortune_archive/2003/10/13/350932/index.htm.

20. Belkin. **initials.** *New York Times*, October 26, 2003, 1.

21. Aven, F. F., Jr., B. Parker, and G.M. McEvoy. "Gender and attitudinal commitment to organizations: A meta-analysis." *Journal of Business Research (*1993) 26: 63-73

22. Winter, D. G. "The power motive in women—and men." *Journal of Personality and Social Psychology,* (1998) 54: 510-519

23. Eagly, A. H., S.J. Karau, M.G. Makhijani. "Gender and the effectiveness of leaders: A meta-analysis." *Psychological Bulletin* (1995) 117: 125-145.

24. "The double-bind dilemma for women in leadership: Damned if you do, doomed if you don't." *Catalyst,* (2007)

25. "The double-bind dilemma for women in leadership: Damned if you do, doomed if you don't." *Catalyst,* (2007)

26. Babcock, L., and Laschever, S. Women Don't Ask. The High Cost of Avoiding Negotiation—and Positive Strategies for Change. (New York: Bantam Books, 2007)

27. Timpson, J. "A Glaring Double Standard,"*Globe and Mail,* March 30, 2009. http://www.theglobeandmail.com/life/article669079.ece

Chapter two

28. Immen, W."Women in top positions on the decline." *Globe and Mail,* January 16, 2007.

29. Shelton, Beth Anne. "The division of household labor," *Annual Review of Sociology* (August 1996): 299-322

30. Jean Fulton "Motivating men and women at work: Relationships vs. rewards, *International Survey Research*. News release, August 3, 2004.

31. Fiorina, Carly. Tough choices. A memoir. (New York: Portfolio: The Penguin Group, 2006)

32. Fiorina, Carly. Tough choices. A memoir. (New York: Portfolio: The Penguin Group, 2006)

33. Timpson, J. "A Glaring Double Standard,"*Globe and Mail,* March 30, 2009. http://www.theglobeandmail.com/life/article669079.ece

34. Packer, George. "The choice," *The New Yorker,* January 2008.

35. Joy, Lois. Advancing women leaders: The connection between women board directors and women corporate officers, *Catalyst,* (2008).

36. 2007 Catalyst Census of Women Board Directors of the Fortune 500, *Catalyst,* (2007); 2007 Catalyst Census of Women Corporate Officers and Top Earners of the Fortune 500, *Catalyst,* (2007); 2006 Catalyst Census of Women Board Directors of the Fortune 500, *Catalyst,* (2006); 2006 Catalyst Census of Women Corporate Officers and Top Earners of the Fortune 500, *Catalyst,* (2006).

37. Joy, Lois. Advancing women leaders: The connection between women board directors and women corporate officers, *Catalyst,* (2008).

38. The Female FTSE Report 2004, Cranfield University School of Management, 2004.

39. "Are women the antidote?" CERAM Business School, http://www.ceram.edu/index.php/News-programs/News-MSc-programs/Global-Financial-Crisis-Are-Women-the-Antidote-CERAM-Research.html.

40. Desvaux, Georges, Devillard-Hoellinger, Sandrine, and Meaney, Mary, C. "A business case for women," *The McKinsey Quarterly* (September 16, 2008).

41. Deszo, Cristia, L., and Gaddis Ross, David. "Girl power: Female participation in top management and firm performance. Working paper, December 2007.

42. Konrad, Alison, M. and Kramer, Vicki, W. "How many women do boards need? *Harvard Business Review*, December 2006.

43. Konrad, Alison, M. and Kramer, Vicki, W. "How many women do boards need?" *Harvard Business Review*, December 2006.

44. "Groundbreakers. Using the strength of women to rebuild the world economy," Ernst & Young (May, 2009) http://www.ey.com/GL/en/Issues/Driving-growth/Groundbreakers---Executive-Summary.

45. Michaels, Ed., Handfield-Jones, Helen., and Axelrod, Beth. The War for Talent (Boston: Harvard Business School Press, 2001).

46. Gutheridge, Matthew., Komm, Asmus, B., and Lawson, Emily. "Making talent a strategic priority." *The McKinsey Quarterly* (September 16, 2008).

47. Gutheridge, Matthew., Komm, Asmus, B., and Lawson, Emily. "Making talent a strategic priority." *The McKinsey Quarterly* (September 16, 2008).

48. Desvaux, Georges., Devillard-Hoellinger, Sandrine., and Meaney, Mary, C. "A business case for women." *The McKinsey Quarterly* (September 16, 2008).

49. Desvaux, Georges., Devillard-Hoellinger, Sandrine., and Meaney, Mary, C. "A business case for women."*The McKinsey Quarterly* (September 16, 2008).

50. The bottom line: Connecting corporate performance and gender diversity. *Catalyst*, (2004).

51. 2007 Catalyst Census of Women Board Directors of the Fortune 500, *Catalyst*, (2007); 2007 Catalyst Census of Women Corporate Officers and Top Earners of the Fortune 500, *Catalyst*, (2007); 2006 Catalyst Census of Women Board Directors of the Fortune 500, *Catalyst*, (2006); 2006 Catalyst Census of

Women Corporate Officers and Top Earners of the Fortune 500, *Catalyst*, (2006).

Chapter three

52. For original change model, see Beckhard, R. Organization development: Strategies and models (Reading, MA: Addison-Wesley, 1969).

53. Prime, Jeanine & Moss-Racusin, Corinne A. Catalyst report: Engaging men in gender initiatives: What change agents need to know. Catalyst, (2009). www.catalyst.org.

54. Robert Hinkley, "How Corporate Law Inhibits Social Responsibility," Business Ethics: Corporate Social Responsibility Report, (January-February, 2002) www.commondreams.org/views02/0119-04.htm

55. European Professional Women's Network and Egon Zehnder International 2008. Third Bi-annual EuropeanPWN BoardWomen, *Monitor,* (2008).   http://www.europeanpwn.net/files/3rd_bwm_2008_press_release_1.pdf.

56. Nebenzahl, Donna. "Utopian Workplace Embraces Feminine Values." *The Montreal Gazette*. September 20, 2008. http://www.working.com/resources/story.html?id=1771e462-c9e5-4723-a1f9-3dbef8454ce3

57. European Professional Women's Network and Egon Zehnder International 2008. Third Bi-annual EuropeanPWN BoardWomen, *Monitor,* (2008).   http://www.europeanpwn.net/files/3rd_bwm_2008_press_release_1.pdf.

58. Toomey, Christine. "Quotas for women on the board: do they work?" *TimesOnLine,* (2008). http://women.timesonline.co.uk/tol/life_and_style/women/article4066740.ece

59. Toomey, Christine. "Quotas for women on the board: do they work?" *TimesOnLine,* (2008). http://women.timesonline.co.uk/tol/life_and_style/women/article4066740.ece

60. Toomey, Christine. "Quotas for women on the board: do they work?" *TimesOnLine,* (2008). http://women.timesonline.co.uk/tol/life_and_style/women/article4066740.ece

61. Toomey, Christine. "Quotas for women on the board: do they work?" *TimesOnLine,* (2008). http://women.timesonline.co.uk/tol/life_and_style/women/article4066740.ece

62. Sweetman, Kate. "Decoding leadership: Norway's boards two years later: What difference do women make?" *FastCompany,* (July 13, 2009). http://www.fastcompany.com/blog/kate-sweetman/decoding-leadership/norway-s-boards-two-years-later-what-difference-do-women-make.

63. "Reverse discrimination," Wikipedia http://en.wikipedia.org/wiki/Reverse_discrimination.

64. Thompson, P. and Graham, J. A woman's place is in the boardroom. (Basingstoke, Hampshire.Palgrave Mamillan, 2005).

65. Toomey, Christine. "Quotas for women on the board: do they work?" *TimesOnLine,* (2008). http://women.timesonline.co.uk/tol/life_and_style/women/article4066740.ece

66. Toomey, Christine. "Quotas for women on the board: do they work?" *TimesOnLine,* (2008). http://women.timesonline.co.uk/tol/life_and_style/women/article4066740.ece

67. Toomey, Christine. "Quotas for women on the board: do they work?" *TimesOnLine,* (2008). http://women.timesonline.co.uk/tol/life_and_style/women/article4066740.ece

68. Toomey, Christine. "Quotas for women on the board: do they work?" *TimesOnLine,* (2008). http://women.timesonline.co.uk/tol/life_and_style/women/article4066740.ece

69. Toomey, Christine. "Quotas for women on the board: do they work?" *TimesOnLine,* (2008). http://women.timesonline.co.uk/tol/life_and_style/women/article4066740.ece

70. 2007 Catalyst Census of Women Board Directors of the Fortune 500, *Catalyst,* (2007); 2007 Catalyst Census of Women Corporate Officers and Top Earners of the Fortune 500, *Catalyst,* (2007); 2006 Catalyst Census of Women Board Directors of the Fortune 500, *Catalyst,* (2006); 2006 Catalyst Census of Women Corporate Officers and Top Earners of the Fortune 500, *Catalyst,* (2006).

Chapter four

71. Catalyst Award Winners. *Catalyst,* http://www.catalyst.org/page/69/catalyst-award-winners.

Chapter five

72. The double-bind dilemma for women in leadership: Damned if you do, doomed if you don't. *Catalyst,* (2007).

73. Clymer, A. "Book Says Nixon Considered a Woman for Supreme Court," *New York Times,* September 27, 2001,.A16 http://query.nytimes.com/gst/fullpage.html?res=9B02EED6103AF934A1575AC0A9679C8B63&sec=&spon=&pagewanted=1.

74. Timpson, J. "A Glaring Double Standard,"*Globe and Mail,* February 26, 2008.

75. Two excellent books demonstrating the impact of women not asking for what they want in salary negotiations are: Women don't ask. The high cost of avoiding negotiation-and positive strategies for change by Linda Babcock and Sara Laschever; and

Getting even. Why women don't get paid like men—and what to do about it by Evelyn Murphy with E. J. Graff.

76. Packer, George. "The choice,"*The New Yorker*, (January 2008).

Chapter six

77. Mackay, Harvey . Dig your well before you're thirsty. (New York: Currency Doubleday, 1997).

78. Gladwell, Malcolm The tipping point. How little things can make a big difference. (Little, Brown and Company, 2000).

79. Nour, David. Relationship economics: Transform your most valuable business contacts into personal and professional success. (Hoboken, New Jersey: John Wiley and Sons, 2008).

80. Ferris, Timothy. The 4-hour workweek: Escape 9-5, live anywhere, and join the new rich. (New York: Crown Publishers, 2007).

Chapter seven

81. ICF Global Coaching Client Study, (February, 2009). http://www. coachfederation.org.

Chapter eight

82. Hewlett, Sylvia Ann. Off-ramps and on-ramps. Keeping talented women on the road to success. (Boston, Massachusetts: Harvard Business School Press, 2007).

83. Gallup study: Feeling good matters in the workplace.(2006). http:// gmj.gallup.com/content/20770/Gallup-Study-Feeling-Good-Matters-in-the.aspx

84. Fritz, Robert. www.robertfriz.com.

85. Fritz, Robert. Your life as art. (Newfane: Newfane Press, 2003).

86. Fritz, Robert. Your life as art. (Newfane: Newfane Press, 2003).

87. Lucy McCauley. "Don't burn out!" *Fast Company Magazine*, (December 19, 2007). www.fastcompany.com/magazine/34/one.html?page=0%2C0.

Chapter nine

88. Kouzes, James, M and Posner, Barry, Z.The Leadership Challenge. Third Ed. (San Francisco: Jossey-Bass, 2002).

89. George, Bill. Authentic Leadership. Rediscovering the Secrets to Creating Lasting Value. (San Francisco: Jossey-Bass. 2003).

90. Goffee, Robert and Jones, Gareth. "The real thing. An interview with Rob Goffee and Gareth Jones". *Business Strategy Review,* (Autumn 2005). http://www.london.edu/assets/documents/publications/The_real_thing__The_art_of_authentic_leadership.pdf

91. Goffee, Robert and Jones, Gareth. "Why should anyone be led by you? *Harvard Business Review*. (September 25, 2000).

92. Fritz, Robert The path of *least* resistance. Learning to become the creative force in your own life. (New York: Fawcett Columbine, 1984).

93. Goffee, Robert and Jones, Gareth. "The real thing. An interview with Rob Goffee and Gareth Jones". *Business Strategy Review,* (Autumn 2005). http://www.london.edu/assets/documents/publications/The_real_thing__The_art_of_authentic_leadership.pdf

Chapter ten

94. Center for Women's Business Research, (2008-2009) http://www.womensbusinessresearchcenter.org/research/keyfacts/

95. Statistics Canada. Key Small Business Statistics, (January 2009). http://www.ic.gc.ca/eic/site/sbrp-rppe.nsf/vwapj/KSBS-PSRPE_ Jan2009_eng.pdf/$FILE/KSBS-PSRPE_Jan2009_eng.pdf.

96. Women's Enterprise Task Force, (2008), http://www.women senterprisetaskforce.co.uk/.

97. Women's Enterprise Task Force, (2008), http://www.women senterprisetaskforce.co.uk/.

98. *Sunday Express*, (March 9, 2008).

99. "Guide to developing a law firm policy regarding accommodation requirements," *Law Society of Upper Canada,* (May 2005).

Recycled
Supporting responsible use
of forest resources
www.fsc.org Cert no. SGS-COC-003153
© 1996 Forest Stewardship Council

Marquis Book Printing Inc.

Québec, Canada
2010

This book has been printed on 100% post consumer
waste paper, certified Eco-logo and processed chlorine free.